BRAND CURRENCY

Brand Currency

A Former Amazon Exec on Money,
Information, Loyalty, and Time

Steve Susi

LIONCREST
PUBLISHING

BRAND CURRENCY

A Former Amazon Exec on Money, Information, Loyalty, and Time

ISBN   978-1-5445-1402-4   *Paperback*
       978-1-5445-1401-7   *Ebook*
       978-1-5445-0308-0   *Audiobook*

To my parents, brothers, and sister, who taught me everything.

Contents

Introduction

"The past is disputed. The present is well out of hand. All that's left is the future."

—UNCLE MILT

Exhale.

As a businessperson and private citizen in this brave new tech world of ours, what you're almost certainly feeling right now is a steamy bouillabaisse of confusion, fear of falling behind, and surreality. Hopefully, there's some wonder and exhilaration in there too, but whatever you're experiencing, the pace of the new techonomy feels like it's accelerating faster every year. That's because it is. We'll get into why in a moment, but suffice it to say, companies like Amazon have simultaneously made life easier in many ways yet harder to understand and keep up with in others.

Complex mathematics that only a handful of human beings can comprehend work invisibly and tirelessly on behalf of the customers, companies, and governments they serve. Computations are valuable, literally and figuratively, as the dawn of cryptocurrency has proven, but just like anything man-made they make errors and can be twisted by nefarious actors with less-than-savory intentions. Apprehension toward the unknown is human nature, and since so much depends on these mysterious calculations—from the electricity needed to run the intricate code recipes to the defense, communication, healthcare, transportation, and myriad other systems which enable us to carry out our pursuits of happiness—we've grown uneasy about our silent, all-powerful partners. The term "ambient computing" is now a thing. We are so surrounded by connected machines that they've come to define our physical environment.

We flesh beings are now thoroughly outnumbered, so we nervously joke amongst ourselves about being their pawns. But are we on the brink of being outthought? In the old days, the fear of machines replacing humans applied only to manual labor. Today, they're giving our cognitive abilities a run. Consider AlphaZero, a program from Alphabet's DeepMind Technologies that made headlines in 2017. The software was given nothing more than the basic rules of chess before taking on Stockfish 8, the reigning computer chess world champ. In 100 matches, AlphaZero went 28-0-72. That's right—it didn't lose once. And do you know how long it took for the program to achieve mastery on its own, without human intervention, by competing against itself before Stockfish 8? All of four hours. Chess is a fusion of art, logic, and psychology, and now that machine learning is getting into the creativity game, we feel a whole new class of anxiety. It can be argued that advancements like these have contributed to the rise of populism in recent years. Politics is one of the last realms where average people enjoy relevance and some semblance of power over the world around them. The ballot box is where the computer only counts the votes but is not counted among them.

Sometimes I wonder if my role at Amazon and the digital agencies I've called home most of my career has contributed to this unease. It's conceivable that the human mind did not evolve to accommodate this much stimulus, yet here I am, overloading it nonetheless. Am I to blame a little bit for this atmosphere of angst? If you work in tech, media, advertising, marketing, branding, design, or another related field, do you ever ask yourself this question? If so, I'd like to believe it's because we know we have a responsibility to do right by our fellow man and woman, so it's probably a good thing we go about our jobs with that lodged in the back of our minds as a sort of moral compass.

When I read of the latest advancements, I'm reminded of a quote from Marshall Berman's 1982 book on the destructive nature of modernization, *All That Is Solid Melts into Air*:

"To be modern is to find ourselves in an environment that promises us adventure, power, joy, growth, transformation of ourselves and the world—and at the same time that threatens to destroy everything we have, everything we know, everything we are."

I'm confident we can build the former and sidestep the latter. Call me altruistic, but we in the business of communicating to customers on behalf of brands can take the first step toward earning heartfelt loyalty with useful information while doing our honest best to save customers time and money. These are the notions that matter to everyone, everywhere, from every walk of life, no matter what "percent" you are.

That's why I decided to write this book.

A brand with power isn't bad. The owner of a brand misusing power certainly is. Money isn't evil either. Greed at the expense of others is. If we as communications professionals are to weather the brand-pocolypse (already underway if you believe the pundits), we must appeal to the core ideals of the customer as a living, breathing—not necessarily spending—individual. That takes the right technology, sure, but more crucially, a customer-first obligation to empathy.

WHAT YOU CAN EXPECT FROM *BRAND CURRENCY*

At Amazon, there are 14 leadership principles (called "LPs").

I'll delve into them soon, but consistently topping inter-national brand equity and reputation surveys for the past decade doesn't happen by accident. It requires a total, willful, enterprise-wide commitment to one thing only. While all LPs are important, one reigns supreme: Customer Obsession is far and away the most critical, period. And if you can't prove you have it top of mind, don't even bother taking your first phone screen with an Amazon recruiter. It's not about you and it never was. As such, this book will serve as a guide to making the customer the core of everything you do.

When you truly, honestly obsess over the customer, you'll begin to understand why a company like General Electric, with a 102-year head start on Amazon, has a market cap of $78.8 billion at the time of this writing, while AMZN's is $818.95 billion, a 939 percent disparity. You might argue my use of market value as evidence of customer obsession, and you'd be right in some ways. However, I would respond with a few points. First, GE was cofounded by, among others, billionaire financier J. P. Morgan and Alexander Graham Bell, the man who invented the telephone and refined the phonograph. Talk about all the resources and technologi-cal advantage in the world. Next, Amazon was founded in a garage by one man, Jeff Bezos, to sell books. How, in less than a quarter-century, has Amazon risen to such promi-nence, while GE has retreated to single-digit stock value? Customer obsession. That's it. That's everything. That's all, folks.

So as we struggle to deal with these turbulent times (when have times not been turbulent?), there actually is no fog. You can exhale again, this time with confidence. The answer's been right in front of you your whole career. To borrow from the mouth of the South, James Carville: it's the customer, stupid. Now of course, you're not stupid, esteemed reader. Businesspeople have simply not been conditioned to work under a mindset in which customers are decision one. I was guilty of it for a year even *after* I started at Amazon. Now, I'm going to show you how that most peculiar company does it—and how you can too.

For nearly six years, I was a creative leader at Amazon Advertising, specifically a group called Advertising Design and User Experience, or "ADX" for short. ADX handles hundreds of clients the world over and builds experiences to engage customers across the Amazon universe. And contrary to Amazon's core reputation as an e-commerce company, the majority of ADX's time was spent creating brand-level campaigns, not e-commerce units. In 2012, I was the first creative director on the ground in ADX's New York City office; a few years later, the first group creative director at ADX globally; and in 2016, its first-ever executive creative director, based in London. During that journey, I transformed from a client-only agency guy who resisted the LPs as corporate hooey, into a customer-first acolyte. I am now firmly converted because I watched it in action. And it works.

But that's only half the story. Because I'd spent my pre-Amazon career on the agency side, servicing clients from Mercedes-Benz and P&G to Gucci and Cadillac, I found myself constantly analyzing the Amazon approach against not just how agencies behave but the ways clients approach their businesses. Additionally, at Amazon, I was fortunate to work with the world's best-known brands across many business sectors in the US, Europe, and Asia. It became apparent that concern over the bottom line and shareholders wasn't just a US thing. It's an every-business thing. (The irony is, in my experience, the more you focus on your shareholders, the less each share is ultimately worth.) For now, I'm here to tell you that Amazon is different when it comes to its customer, which is why its success is different.

Ask the former leaders of Toys "R" Us, Radio Shack, Blockbuster, Circuit City, and Borders what they'd have done differently. I suspect many would respond with some form of "We should've paid more attention to the customer." Somewhere between Amazon and the dustbin of business history are 99 percent of all companies. Chances are you work for one now. Odds are also decent that your company started before 1994. What's the difference then? What courses through Amazon's veins that's so unique?

To help me make sense of and explain to others what I learned at Amazon, a system occurred to me one day in 2014 based on the recurring themes I saw and heard every hour of each workday. It became clear after a few years that the LPs, programs, and individual and team goals always mapped back to the customer's money, information, loyalty, or time. While also important, Amazon's money, information, loyalty, and time were permanently second in priority. Without this company—or any other, for that matter—behaving that way toward itself, it can never act in kind outwardly, as I'll prove throughout these pages.

And then, an epiphany. It was these properties—these *currencies*—that Amazon and its customers exchanged on a continual basis that jumped out and were made self-evident. As I moved through my career there, I fixated on the concept, capturing and analyzing examples as they took place in real time, following them to conclusion. Our brains are mere value exchanges, gray-matter trading desks, and understanding and respecting these currencies were the secrets to Amazon's success. This is what I want to share with you, because the approach and the techniques driving it can be applied to any organization—multinational or mom-and-pop, young or old, public or private.

In fact, they're more than keys to brand success. Money, information, loyalty, and time are human truths, the ancient media of our existence, pillars of our species' development, the legacies of our race. They are the fundamental inputs and outputs of the human condition. Living according to their rules is what separates us from other animals and what distinguishes great brands from the rest.

In this book, I attempt to explain each currency in depth as the core mortal foundation it is, detailing each one's origin and evolution to its modern state. Then I take a look at the ways the customer earns and spends them and, finally, how brands do the same, illustrating with anecdotes from my Amazon experience and miniature case studies from around the brandscape along the way. Plus, I present examples of how multiplying currencies is a powerful practice and effective tactic for expediting the elevation of your brand's equity. When you combine all four on behalf of the customer, you will never go wrong.

Understanding it is easy. Getting there won't be, so let's dive into what we're up against.

PART I

—

Pillars

CHAPTER 1

How We Got Here

"Even the scientists could not have predicted the trajectory of these satellites."

—UNCLE MILT

As we approach the age of the zettabyte (that's one sextillion bytes, or a billion terabytes), the information to which we have access is downright dizzying. It amounts to 9.25925926-to-the-ninth-power worth of ones and zeros for every person ever born, if you subscribe to the Population Reference Bureau's estimate of 108 billion *Homo sapiens* who have ever roamed the planet. So you're hardly a wimp if you find your chest tightening anymore, both in business and personal life, when routinely encountering something new that was flat-out impossible a few years or even months ago.

Everyone who participates in modern life has contributed to and taken from these data, and now we find ourselves in a liminal moment. Per the *Oxford English Dictionary*, liminality is defined as "Of or relating to a transitional or intermediate state between culturally defined stages of a person's life, esp. as marked by a ritual or rite of passage." In marital terms, technology is, at this very moment, in the act of carrying us over the threshold, but we're not in the bridal suite just yet, so we feel disoriented, left to openly ponder the future and our place in it.

More data exist with every passing moment than the one prior. Two more people are born per minute than die, all of whom generate information, and I won't even pretend to know what our algorithm-based systems add to the corpus of global data every 60 seconds. Of course, no single machine can process it all (not until quantum computing), let alone we puny humans, so we tend to pick and choose from the stuff that makes us comfortable, that validates our existing perspectives and reinforces our take on society around us. I know I'm guilty of it. Unsurprisingly, this enables, nay, *encourages* us to ignore everything else because trying to parse that much information would require immense effort, and the stuff we'd encounter almost certainly risks us some discomfort. Long gone are the days of so few media outlets that there existed one national conversation through mutual cultural events—when everyone in 1941 from New Mexico to New Hampshire asked if Joltin' Joe extended his hitting streak today. Plus, stretching our mental horizons has lost its appeal because everything we enjoy is instantly presented at the touch of illuminated glass. Why spend my finite energy processing new ideas when I can have a machine justify the views I already have?

TECHSPLOSION

By 2007, tools for content creation gave way to those for content consumption. The great democratization of media would alter the brandscape forever, as the balance of power shifted from major corporations to the individual who could now vote with her thumbs. Suddenly, there were limitless content channels and devices with which to devour them. Just think back to that point of inflection and what a magical year it was—in particular its most notable event, Apple's release of the iPhone. While it wasn't the first smartphone, its processing power, storage, versatility, and app ecosystem are credited with firing the first real starting gun of the mobile revolution. In June, Dropbox was founded, enabling a giant leap in swift, secure digital collaboration. That same year, Google stood on the precipice of delivering Android—the OS that would go on to run 90 percent of the world's smartphones—just 10 months after the search giant purchased YouTube for $1.65 billion, giving everyone on earth their own TV channel and exploding creativity in video. Finally, that November, Amazon launched the Kindle e-reader, irrevocably revolutionizing the publishing industry.

It's important to note that all of those advancements came

on the heels of 2006, itself a seminal year, when Facebook and Twitter went live (but really didn't hit their stride until 2007); Amazon Web Services (AWS) opened its doors, for which nine years later *The Atlantic* would gush, "It's not an understatement to say that AWS is the piece of infrastructure that has enabled the current tech boom"; and Apache released Hadoop, a suite of open-source utilities designed to crunch massive amounts of unstructured data, which played a substantial role in the growth of cloud computing.

In a matter of 24 months, the fractal geometry of the media world multiplied a hundredfold and the on-demand society was set permanently into motion, making for a 24-nanosecond news cycle, galaxies of echo chambers beckoning us, instant gratification becoming the rule, and the nail in the coffin of the homogeneous marketing macroaudience. The community fragmentation that ensued was enabled by devices and algorithms; not surprisingly, it is the algorithm that helps us advertisers "stitch" audiences back together again using purchase and behavioral data.

No wonder we're dizzy. More than a decade later, we find ourselves accelerating toward the physical limits of the processor, as technologies interlock with other technologies, people with other people, and people with technologies, resulting in shorter and shorter development cycles. In 1965, Intel cofounder Gordon Moore predicted in a white paper that the number of transistors in a semiconductor circuit would double every two years while the cost would be halved. Not forever, mind you, but until we hit what is known as the von Neumann bottleneck—that is, when today's computer architecture reaches its ceiling due to the processor's ability versus data transfer rates. Until quantum or neuromorphic computing or something else entirely comes along, we'll continue to drive closer to the chip's borders. If we've known about doubling processing power for more than 50 years, I wonder how we're stupefied at all that we've arrived exactly here.

A NEW YET FAMILIAR ODYSSEY

The composition of this book began in April 2018, 50 years to the month after the release of author Arthur C. Clarke's and director Stanley Kubrick's prescient sci-fi masterpiece *2001: A Space Odyssey*. In that movie, the spacecraft's operations are managed by HAL 9000, a computer that is "incapable of error." (It's rumored that Clarke named it after the three letters preceding "IBM," but Kubrick countered that theory with "HAL" being an acronym for *heuristic* and *algorithmic*). Without spoiling the film for those who haven't seen it, let's just say that humans had created technology capable of making its own decisions, which may or may not threaten those aboard the ship. Did Clarke, a bona fide genius, get the year wrong? Should he have chosen 2007 instead?

Now, I do believe all of this came about under genuinely good intentions. It's what humans do. We try to make things better. We invent to make life easier, even though that sometimes drags unintended consequences along with it. In any case, the technological advancements of the mid-2000s don't amount to a hill of bytes without interconnectivity. Depending on your age, you probably already know the origins of the most impactful tech development of our time, the internet. If you do, please indulge me—and some of the younger folks reading this book who have never known life without it—for a few minutes.

Starting at the US Military's Advanced Research Projects Agency, or ARPA, the ARPANET was a humble, packet-switching network which came to life on four university computers in 1969. (The organization's name was augmented with "Defense" in 1971; thus, you've no doubt heard "DAR-PANET.") The concept was elegant: break information into small pieces called "packets" and disseminate them individually on different paths to be reconstituted back to their original whole at the destination. It was so conceived to allow the military to send and receive information agnostically over multiple communication lines in a national emergency or war instead of over one dedicated conduit which could be easily compromised. If a network line were cut, a packet would always have thousands of other paths to its target.

In the '80s, development of DARPANET was transferred to the then-new Defense Data Network as well as a framework of academic and scientific computers called NSFNet. By the mid-'90s, NSFNet in turn handed over vBNS (the web's "backbone") to a group of commercial carriers and providers, including AGIS-Net99, ANS/AOL, MCI, PSINet, Sprint, and UUNET. The internet as we know it today opened up to Joe Six-Pack in 1991, and it was then that scientists threw the keys to people like me in possession of a 14.4 baud modem and an Apple Quadra, with which I started the web department at my first ad agency, Young Isaac (may it rest in peace) in Columbus, Ohio, as a junior copywriter in 1995.

Before I graduated college two years prior, I signed up to spend an hour on the "Inter-Net." You had to have an Information Technology grad assistant accompany you to explain how it worked, what protocols were, and basic etiquette. He took me to a NeXT computer—that's the company Steve Jobs started after the Apple board dismissed him as CEO in 1985—in the research lab, which awaited me with a pale green cursor flashing slowly. I will never forget the exhilaration of hearing for the first time the growling dial-up connection that sounded like two robots in coitus and seeing the interface appear, scan line by scan line, on the CRT monitor.

"What do you want to do?" my chaperone asked.

"What *can* I do?"

"Well, for starters," he said in geek monotone, "you can type messages to people at other universities using the same software."

"Right now?" I blurted.

He chuckled. "Yeah, right now."

Oh that's definitely what I want to try, I thought, and then proceeded to spend the next 56 minutes trash-talking college football with a student at Wisconsin. I don't think I blinked for the rest of the day. I was hooked, head over heels, gobsmacked. In one month, I would earn my degree in advertising (technically, mass communication with a double concentration in advertising and video production), and all I could think was the Inter-Net just *had* to be the next frontier. No one was talking about an advertising use-case for this "virtual world" yet, but it was obvious to me even then, and I set about learning as much as possible by hoovering up issues of *Wired* and *Internet* and other tech rags.

I remember the summer after graduation telling my parents that I wanted to go into "computer advertising." Little did I know that, a quarter-century on, the advancements in machines, networks, and switching technologies, which now make those early days feel like an episode of *Andy Griffith*, would come as a direct result of advertising budgets. The state of today's web has those old, annoying pop-up banners to thank, just as radio and TV did the 30-second spots before it. Wherever there's content drawing eye- or earballs in the US and most of the world, there are advertising or subscription dollars paying for it. So what was readily apparent to me back then would be ultimately realized at scale within roughly a decade. And most of it was built to sell stuff, which is as American as ARPANET and AOL.

THE INFORMATION SUPERHIGHWAY, THEN AND NOW

Back to the algorithm. As advertisers here in the States jumped on board the burgeoning digital landscape to hawk their wares, it wouldn't be long until the need to track campaign performance and maximize efficiency became the ambition of research and development. In 1996, a Netscape engineer invented the cookie and, two years later, DoubleClick released Boomerang, widely considered the first instance of automated ad retargeting.

I was there, literally. DoubleClick was my client during its early years when I was ACD at independent agency Digital Pulp in New York. DoubleClick had a few dozen employees at the time, but with all the money they'd soon earn for being able to chase people around the web to hit them over and over again with ad impressions—and its eventual acquisition by Google—the small ad-tech company grew into a juggernaut. Ad dollars for the win once again.

Today, retargeting is the bane of most web users' existence, especially now that it's powered by machine learning at companies like LiveRamp. People complain of the "creep factor" of the ad "knowing" what they do online and, later, are repelled by the banner's incessant reappearance, vowing to never shop that site again on principle. This is but one of many symptoms of the growing mistrust of customers toward big brands and the corporations that own them. The deep pockets of corporate America are essentially saying, "This is our internet. We have all the money. If you want to use it, you have to do our bidding and submit to our commercial whims." These brands are using our personal information to nag us into submission and buy the damn shoes. We neither understand nor appreciate it, but we're resigned to allowing it because, well, who are we to fight it?

Our treatment as a target market contributes to widespread suspicion of these technologies and the brand owners that deploy them for capitalistic and often selfish impulses. On November 30, 1999, protesters to the tune of 40,000 amassed outside the Washington State Convention and Trade Center in downtown Seattle as the World Trade Organization gathered for a round of trade negotiations ahead of the new millennium. Nothing short of total chaos ensued. Those indelible images of protesters in gas masks getting shot at with rubber bullets and pepper-sprayed by a small army in paramilitary riot gear (paid for by the taxpayer) shook me and many others. The rally, planned by organizers around the world for months, erupted in response to the uncertainty of globalism and the secretive corporate giants, governments, and banks effectively controlling the world. A dozen years later, Occupy Wall Street would take up residence in Zuccotti Park in New York's Financial District—no more than 20 feet from my office doors when I worked at American Express—to tell the world, "We are the 99 percent," in protest of income inequality. Big companies and their big brands had become big targets.

While those two demonstrations have long since disbanded, a strong undercurrent of mistrust remains. The technologies built to market vitamins to your parents are the same ones distributing hate speech and fake news. Algorithms are amazing with numbers but don't do a thing for empathy; built to give answers but wholly unable to ask questions. When algorithms go sideways, the results can be benign, like the Samsung TV wall mount listed for $1 trillion when Amazon code strings once got locked in a hyper-argument, or malignant, when FBI facial recognition software helps send an innocent person to jail. We sometimes feel out of control of our own lives, and the people and organizations that are much, much richer than we'll ever be are perceived to be making the calls that stand to benefit the 1 percent to our detriment. Accurate or not, the news spouts reports that we don't even have control over the information *about* our own lives, what "they" know about "us," much less if we're being manipulated by some Geppetto data master in the cloud.

There's only one way to avoid joining that crucible of suspicion: recognize and obey the currencies of your customer first and foremost. To that end, let's now take a look at the one brand I believe has earned the highest honors in the disciplines of money, information, loyalty, and time. Take a big fat guess.

CHAPTER 2

Lessons from the Inside

"Not by mirrors but voices is one confidently guided."

—UNCLE MILT

It took me all of two weeks to have my rear end handed to me for the first, and certainly not the last, time at Amazon. Coming from the agency world, I was programmed to start with yes when responding to a client request and then figure out how to fulfill it. One always starts in the affirmative. So when a major financial services (FinServ) client asked ADX to—wait for it—make its logo bigger throughout the customer experience they had sponsored, I naturally obliged. I asked the designer handling the campaign to make the updates and submit them to the product manager in Seattle. About ten minutes later, I got a call.

"Steve, what do you think you're doing?"

"Uh, scaling the logo up 20 percent as the client asked?"

"Well you'd better get something straight," she shot back. "This is not the la-la-land of a digital agency. When a client, big-bucks FinServ or otherwise, asks to make the logo bigger, you tell them, 'Let me check with the product owner.' You're ruining the customer experience. Now go back to your clients and tell them no."

I could hear her breathing as I sat at my desk in stunned silence, eyes open for three full seconds. "OK. Sorry about that. I just thought—"

"I know what you thought," she said. "Fix it." Click. Dial tone.

That was my first conversation with this woman, and while it was a harsh initial impression, it was an awakening and a turning point in my career. I mean, tell clients they can't have something? That would earn you your walking papers on the outside, but not at Amazon. The commitment to the customer experience is total. So I had to call my client with the news that the logo would indeed not be bigger. I remember them not sounding all that surprised.

CUSTOMERS, CUSTOMERS EVERYWHERE

At Amazon, everyone is your customer, not just the millions of shoppers, viewers, listeners, and readers visiting its various domains. ADX's primary internal customers are the sales team members of Amazon Media Group. Your manager is your customer, as are your external clients. The account execs and project managers are customers too. So is the woman who gave me an earful on the phone. If you find yourself, as a corporate employee, visiting a customer service or fulfillment center, those personnel are your customers for as long as you're in the building. The entire culture is one of modest servitude. Colleagues' and clients' feedback is captured as the Voice of the Customer (VOC), a component of most reporting narratives written every day and performance reviews each semester. VOCs typically provide the final section of these documents ahead of the appendix as a humanistic sign-off before the reader dives into metrics.

Does your company listen this intently to the customer? To be perfectly honest, I've never seen another organization come close. After years of VOCs, it appeared to me that there are "mirror companies" and "window companies." Status quo organizations look into mirrors for where to go next, while the remaining few look out the window at the customer. Mirrors are self-important; windows are humble.

Oh, and a quick note on those narrative documents: they are the dominant medium at the company worldwide, and it's on purpose. Bezos, we were told, despises the PowerPoint presentations so pervasive throughout the corporate sphere, and early on, he decided to replace them with one-pagers, two-pagers, and six-pagers, depending on the volume of content needed. All management meetings start in abject silence as everyone reads the same content at the same time—sometimes for as long as 45 minutes for a two-hour quarterly business review. These documents are loaded with information about the customer, internal operations, headcount (officially termed Butts in Seats or "BIS"), and all else that's critical to the business and pertinent to the audience on hand. This way, everyone starts with the latest information, ensuring the remainder of the time is spent at maximum informed efficiency. If you dial in to a conference call and no one's speaking, you learn quickly to mute your phone and start reading the doc, usually sent out a moment before the meeting starts (so that no one reads ahead and all have the freshest information at precisely the same time). It's just one of the many nuances that makes this company so distinct.

A BRIEF HISTORY OF AMAZON

If you don't know the story of this atypical entity named after earth's largest river, allow me to provide a short summary. While at New York City programmatic trading house D. E. Shaw—one of the first Wall Street firms to register a URL in 1992, a full four years before Morgan Stanley—Jeff Bezos came up with the concept of "The Everything Store" after leading the development of the early webmail service Juno and Farsight Financial Services, a sort of ancestor to E-Trade, at Shaw in the early '90s. While immersed in bringing those businesses to life, Bezos read data in a newsletter called *The Matrix News* in 1994 that showed the growth of the World Wide Web was jaw-dropping. With the increase in the transfer of bytes on the internet well into four-digit-percentage territory, he calculated that web activity had grown by a factor of 230,000 percent in the trailing 12 months and was later quoted as saying, "Things just don't grow that fast."

We know now he was spot on. Pumped with early-bird conviction, he left his high-paying job on the Street in the middle of the year—forgoing his annual bonus, which no one does—and put New York in the rearview. It happened so fast he didn't know where they were going to end up, so he told the moving company to pack up his Upper West Side apartment and drive everything West until he called them with an actual destination. Then he hopped a flight to Fort Worth with wife MacKenzie and borrowed his dad's '88 Chevy Blazer. She took the wheel and pointed it Northwest as he typed business plan projections into an Excel doc from the passenger seat.

They decided on Seattle, which is loaded with tech talent. Just ten miles separates Microsoft's headquarters in Redmond from the University of Washington's computer science pipeline. Plus, Washington State's population was relatively small, which made for low sales tax. Jeff was 31. MacKenzie was 24.

When the couple arrived in the suburb of Bellevue, they converted their uninsulated garage (evidently a mandatory for any US tech success story) into an office, famously situating around a black potbelly stove two desks Bezos fashioned out of $60 blonde wood doors he picked up from Home Depot. To this day, all desks at Amazon are made out of the same wood and called "door desks." Check out the cover of this book for what mine looked like.

A store that sells everything would have to start with something. Bezos analyzed 20 product categories, including software, music, and office supplies but landed on books, pure commodities which are easy to ship. Another plus for Seattle was its proximity to a massive book distribution center belonging to one of the two giants of the industry, Ingram, a six-hour drive away in Rosewood, Oregon.

The rest is history (one you can buy at Amazon). From these meager beginnings grew the highest wealth ever accumulated by an individual, estimated at $161.7 billion at the time of this writing. Consider again General Electric, which had the inexhaustible backing of financial tycoon John Pierpont Morgan, whose fortune historians in 2007 appraised at $38 billion in adjusted dollars. Bezos financed the first phase of what began as Cadabra.com with $10,000 of his own money, and then another $84,000 in interest-free bank loans. (Cadabra was often mistaken for "cadaver" over the phone, so the name was thankfully dropped.)

One quote explains the diverging trajectories of those two companies, and it came from computer scientist Alan Kay, whom the young entrepreneur looked up to: "A point of view is worth 80 IQ points." I heard it repeated often during my time with the company, and it speaks clearly to the inner workings of Jeff Bezos. To me, it says if you thoroughly believe your objective is right by the customer, have the data to back it up, and never waiver come what may, success is all but guaranteed for anyone with even a reasonable intellect.

Case in point: in 1995, Bezos received a letter from an angry publishing exec, castigating him for allowing customers to post negative reviews of his and other imprints' titles. Just as the product manager who was less than enthused about my prospect of a larger logo, Jeff's reaction must have been equal parts annoyance and indifference. It would be natural for the average businessperson to feel like they've let down a partner upon whom his company's growth depends, but just as in the FinServ example, Amazon is not in the business of prioritizing other companies over the customer—any customer, at any time. You will see examples of this principle throughout the book, and I don't see that ever changing. Ask yourself, "What would the CEO of my company do? Call and apologize, or deposit it into the nearest recycling bin?" "Customer trust at all costs" is the ultimate outmaneuver at Amazon.

If only the dyspeptic publisher had the chance to read Amazon's first letter to its shareholders in 1997—two years after he sent his note—to see why his appeal was sent in vain. The first bullet under the "It's All About the Long Term" heading reads, "We will continue to focus relentlessly on our customers." The operative word here is "relentlessly." I am here to tell you that it is a nonstop, every-move-you-make proposition at Amazon. It is not corporate mission-speak, and it's anything but hollow. It's chiefly what Amazonians are hired, developed, promoted, and terminated against. After Cadabra.com was thrown out, and before settling on Amazon.com, Bezos considered Relentless.com for the company name. For further proof, enter Relentless.com into a web browser right now and see where you land. That's right: it redirects you to Amazon.com. The young CEO knew before the first line of code was written that this would be his approach to the business.

Taking this line of thinking a step further, paying attention to competitors is a cultural taboo at Amazon. Why spend valuable time and energy on a rival when you could focus on the customer instead? At a 1997 all-hands meeting, when an employee asked about the lawsuit filed by Barnes & Noble over Amazon's book-selling claims, Bezos responded, "Don't be worried about our competitors because they're never going to send us any money anyway. Let's be worried about our customers and stay heads-down focused." It felt to me that the mere mention of a competitor's name was seen as a sign of weakness. How much time do you spend worrying about or even emulating your competition where you work?

It may sound difficult, but forgetting that you have competitors is astonishingly easy. Just zoom your cultural lens as far in on the customer as you can and watch the competition, shareholders, and all other distractions disappear outside the frame.

In 2011, five major publishing houses filed a lawsuit against Amazon for its $9.99 e-book prices, far too deep a discount for their tastes. "Fortunately for the publishers," charged Hagens Berman attorney Steve Berman, "they had a co-conspirator as terrified as they were over Amazon's popularity and pricing structure, and that was Apple." I absolutely love that line because within it sits Amazon's singular customer obsession. These companies—even almighty Apple—were "terrified" about Amazon's "popularity" with its customers. The case against Amazon was soon dropped, at which point the US Justice Department turned its sights on the publishers and Apple, whom it saw as engaging in a conspiracy to violate federal antitrust laws. The tech giant was ultimately ordered to pay $450 million as part of a settlement in 2016. On April 11, 2012, Ylan Q. Mui and Hayley Tsukayama of the *Washington Post* reported, "The government painted a portrait of an industry desperately trying to turn a profit amid rapid changes in technology and aggressive competition from online retailers. In phone conversations, e-mails and dinners at exclusive New York restaurants, the companies' top executives colluded to wrest control of the market from Amazon.com and raise prices on e-books, according to the complaint." I hope the conspirators at least ordered the surf and turf.

PROUDLY PECCY

Amazon knows it is peculiar and embraces the truth wholly. In fact, the internal mascot (a little orange creature seen littering my door desk on the back cover of this book) is named "Peccy," short for "peculiar."

What is genuinely intriguing to most people is the vast range of Amazon's businesses. Because of this, I used to start ADX pitches and capabilities presentations with, "Welcome to Amazon, the company that delivers your bananas in two hours for free, provides cloud computing and storage for governments, and just won three Academy Awards. We are not normal, and your experience with our creative teams won't be either."

How did a company that in 1994 drove packages of book orders to the Bellevue post office in the back of a Honda become so dominant in these and many other seemingly unrelated arenas? The answer is a matter of perspective, and the keyword is "seemingly."

"THE EVERYTHING STORE"

In addition to its core e-commerce offering dealing hundreds of millions of items from nearly every conceivable product category on their owned and operated sites—as well as millions more via Fulfillment by Amazon (FBA)—let's take a look at just a portion of their portfolio, starting with the basics. Books are available in physical, digital, and audio formats, as are music, movies, and TV shows from services like Amazon Books, Goodreads, Audible, Brilliance Audio, AbeBooks, Amazon Music, Music Unlimited, Prime Music, and Prime Video. Okay, so you knew that.

But did you know it's also a freight and logistics company (Amazon Air, Amazon Maritime, Prime Air, Beijing Century Joyo Courier Services, Amazon Locker, the aforementioned FBA), grocery store (AmazonFresh, Prime Pantry, Whole Foods Market), hardware manufacturer (Lab126, Kindle, Fire Tablet, Fire TV, Fire TV Stick, Dash Button, Dash Wand, Alexa devices), video content creation company (Amazon Studios, Storybuilder), cloud computing provider (Amazon Web Services, Amazon Drive), gaming design and media provider (Amazon Game Studios, Twitch, Lumberyard, Amazon Digital Game Store), robotics company (Amazon Robotics, Kiva Systems), search technology developer (A9), and advertising company (Amazon Advertising)? It owns the world's largest movie database (IMDb), cloud-based comic book store (ComiXology), and online shoe retailer (Zappos). Did you know it offers 3D body modeling (Body Labs), data visualization services (Graphiq), and pharmaceuticals (Pill Pack), and is a startup incubator (Launchpad), home improvement services provider (Amazon Home Services), and fashion designer (Franklin & Freeman, Franklin Tailored, James & Erin, Lark & Ro, North Eleven, Scout + Ro, Society New York, Goodsport, Rebel Canyon, and Peak Velocity)? You probably didn't.

And that just scratches the surface. Notice I didn't even mention Prime Now, the ultrafast delivery service which digital research firm L2's Scott Galloway calculated has more subscribers in the US than go to church every week, still have a landline, or own a firearm. How can that all be from the same company, and one that did it in less than 25 years at that? Furthermore, what do all of them have in common anyway? Simple. They all have a customer to better satisfy.

Despite the media's depiction as a serial disruptor, Amazon is not out to wreck other businesses in some weird corporate winner-take-all deathmatch. Fans of TV's *Star Trek: The Next Generation* know the Borg, a cybernetic collective of aliens and technologies resembling a gigantic black Rubik's Cube. The Borg roams the galaxy, robotically conquering and assimilating whatever's in its way (except the Enterprise, of course), absorbing all the knowledge and consciousness of its prey—sometimes a spacecraft, other times a planet—which in turn makes the Collective even more powerful and harder to stop. In the film *Star Trek: First Contact*, it transmits this warning to Captain Jean-Luc Picard and his crew: "We are the Borg. Lower your shields and surrender your ships.

We will add your biological and technological distinctiveness to our own. Your culture will adapt to service us. Resistance is futile."

Contrary to popular myth, Amazon is no Borg. In fact, I've come up with another, more apt analogy. Think of this company as a smartphone, where leadership principles are the operating system, programs are the features and functions, goals are the apps, and the customer is the battery. (The irony of this metaphor is not lost on me, what with the Amazon Fire Phone as Amazon's best-known miscue.) Amazon simply uses data, analytics, and insights to find areas where a *customer experience stands to be improved*. With customers seen as the power-source for its entire operation, the company spends every ounce of effort seeking ways to recharge them, to make them last longer. It's as straightforward as that. Amazon is not, nor will it ever be, a disruptor. "Disruptive" is how *other businesses* describe this or any other company that dethrones them.

It's hardly Amazon's fault that other businesses aren't doing their best by their customers. Indeed, it should be every company's prime objective to relentlessly find and fix problems on behalf of them. This is the sole reason behind Amazon's existence. Remind yourself by reentering Relentless.com into your browser. To the customer—whom I hope I've firmly established by this point is the only thing that matters and remains the object of all of Amazon's attentions—low prices, speedy delivery, and wide selection are not "disruptive." Flat tires and summer colds are disruptive. To the customer, convenience, selection, reliability, and low prices are common sense.

THE 14 LEADERSHIP PRINCIPLES

Let's start at the top with the LPs. If you've been curious about Amazon for some time and have done your due diligence, there's nothing new here. If you haven't or just want to refresh your memory, here they are, pulled right from their publicly facing jobs site.*

CUSTOMER OBSESSION

Leaders start with the customer and work backwards. They work vigorously to earn and keep customer trust. Although leaders pay attention to competitors, they obsess over customers.

OWNERSHIP

Leaders are owners. They think long term and don't sacrifice long-term value for short-term results. They act on behalf of the entire company, beyond just their own team. They never say, "that's not my job."

---

*   "Amazon's Global Career Site." Amazon.jobs. Accessed January 15, 2019. https://www.amazon.jobs/en/principles.

INVENT AND SIMPLIFY

Leaders expect and require innovation and invention from their teams and always find ways to simplify. They are externally aware, look for new ideas from everywhere, and are not limited by "not invented here." As we do new things, we accept that we may be misunderstood for long periods of time.

ARE RIGHT, A LOT

Leaders are right a lot. They have strong judgment and good instincts. They seek diverse perspectives and work to disconfirm their beliefs.

LEARN AND BE CURIOUS

Leaders are never done learning and always seek to improve themselves. They are curious about new possibilities and act to explore them.

HIRE AND DEVELOP THE BEST

Leaders raise the performance bar with every hire and promotion. They recognize exceptional talent, and willingly move them throughout the organization. Leaders develop leaders and take seriously their role in coaching others. We work on behalf of our people to invent mechanisms for development like Career Choice.

INSIST ON THE HIGHEST STANDARDS

Leaders have relentlessly high standards—many people may think these standards are unreasonably high. Leaders are continually raising the bar and drive their teams to deliver high quality products, services, and processes. Leaders ensure that defects do not get sent down the line and that problems are fixed so they stay fixed.

THINK BIG

Thinking small is a self-fulfilling prophecy. Leaders create and communicate a bold direction that inspires results. They think differently and look around corners for ways to serve customers.

BIAS FOR ACTION

Speed matters in business. Many decisions and actions are reversible and do not need extensive study. We value calculated risk-taking.

FRUGALITY

Accomplish more with less. Constraints breed resourcefulness, self-sufficiency and invention. There are no extra points for growing headcount, budget size, or fixed expense.

EARN TRUST

Leaders listen attentively, speak candidly, and treat others respectfully. They are vocally self-critical, even when doing so is awkward or embarrassing. Leaders do not believe their or their team's body odor smells of perfume. They benchmark themselves and their teams against the best.

DIVE DEEP

Leaders operate at all levels, stay connected to the details, audit frequently, and are skeptical when metrics and anecdote differ. No task is beneath them.

HAVE BACKBONE; DISAGREE AND COMMIT

Leaders are obligated to respectfully challenge decisions when they disagree, even when doing so is uncomfortable or exhausting. Leaders have conviction and are tenacious. They do not compromise for the sake of social cohesion. Once a decision is determined, they commit wholly.

DELIVER RESULTS

Leaders focus on the key inputs for their business and deliver them with the right quality and in a timely fashion. Despite setbacks, they rise to the occasion and never settle.

LPs AND THE FOUR CURRENCIES

As I see it, these principles all map to the four currencies in multiple ways. Here's another look at them aligned with money, information, loyalty, and time.

MONEY

- **Frugality:** Minimizing operating expenses leads to lower costs for the customer (for instance, no one, not even executives, are allowed to fly any class but coach unless they want to pay the difference themselves). This keeps you humble and ensures you remember that the customer gets the perks, not the employee.

INFORMATION

- **Are Right, A Lot:** Come to every meeting armed with data to support your convictions and assertions for bets to place with minimum budget.
- **Learn and Be Curious:** Consume and retain as many new perspectives as you can and employ them on behalf of a diverse customer population.
- **Dive Deep:** Go well below surface information and seek an outcome's root causes so you can replicate or avoid it in the future.
- **Deliver Results:** Fulfill your goals. If you cannot produce data as evidence of your actions, it never happened.

LOYALTY

- **Customer Obsession:** I need not explain this one again.
- **Ownership:** Sweating the details and leaving no stone unturned shows you care about the result and, by proxy, the customer.
- **Hire and Develop the Best:** Every person hired, as well as their professional development—whether or not you manage them—is a gesture of customer devotion.
- **Insist on the Highest Standards:** People you love are almost certainly Amazon customers. Do as well as you would for them in all you do, and continue to improve.
- **Think Big:** Imagine unexpected ways to earn even more customer satisfaction. The bigger and hairier, the better.
- **Earn Trust:** Success starts and ends with customer trust, particularly when it comes to protecting their data, and don't forget that everyone's your customer.
- **Have Backbone; Disagree and Commit:** If you believe there's a better way to do something for the customer or Amazon, you are expected to respectfully raise your concern after constructing a plan—supported by data—to initiate and own.

TIME

- **Invent and Simplify:** If it takes as long or longer—or it's more complex—for anyone internally or externally, to achieve the same result offered by the previous system, it's not an innovation.

- **Bias for Action:** Take the initiative without having to be ordered to do something that improves the customer experience or company. Usually, having 70 percent of the data is enough to make an informed decision.
- **Frugality:** This one appears twice because wasting a fellow employee's time with a poorly planned meeting or unnecessary email directly translates into a slower innovation cycle and ultimately raises prices.

HIRING AND RAISING THE BAR

Unbeknownst to me, in 2012, I was hired against these principles. While I prepared ardently and read as much about interviewing at Amazon as I could, I don't recall finding anything online more than sample questions and admonitions that successful candidates need to go in with a "challenge, approach, solution, results" framework. Evidently, what I did on Valentine's Day that year worked, but if I'd have known just how deeply the LPs were ingrained into the questions themselves, the job description, the prebrief, the interview day (called a "loop"), and the debrief, I'd have spent all my time on those and worked them into my preparation.

A little more on the loop. It is sternly serious business at Amazon, as demonstrated by the Hire and Develop the Best LP. Every loop requires at least four hours of each hiring manager's (HM) time: a one-hour phone screen, a half-hour prebrief, a one-hour on-site interview, one hour to complete and submit the notes taken during the loop into the recruiting system, and a half-hour debrief, where the decision is made. All Amazonians in the loop who are not the hiring manager share the same responsibilities apart from the phone screen, which belongs to the HM and one other senior, trusted teammate. It's called a loop because the candidate cycles through six employees, which takes the entire day (with an hour for lunch). All but one person involved hold positions related to the job on offer, and none of them can be below the level of the role being filled.

The last person remaining is the Bar-Raiser (BR), who often comes from a completely unrelated organization ("org"). In Brad Stone's exhaustive 2014 account of the company and its enigmatic CEO, *The Everything Store: Jeff Bezos and the Age of Amazon*, I learned that the BR was inspired by an interviewing method employed at D. E. Shaw and that Bezos brought the concept with him. The Bar-Raiser program is in place to prevent the gradual decay of the company's personnel standards as Amazon grows.

A BR is an employee in good standing who's been there at least a few years, demonstrates the LPs in their everyday performance, and has a proven eye for top talent. There must be one BR in each loop (sometimes they bring a BR-in-training to shadow), and their primary job is to ensure the candidate raises the bar—is better than 50 percent of the existing employees in that org—as judged against the LPs in addition to their work experience, technical acumen, and communication skills. Since the BR frequently comes from a different org, he or she will ask questions about the organization in the prebrief and debrief to help the group determine if this person does in fact raise the bar. Each looper can choose from four different verdicts: Strong Hire, Inclined to Hire, Not Inclined to Hire, and Strong No Hire. In my 300+ loops, I rarely saw a BR's "Not Inclined" overruled, and never once saw a BR's "Strong No Hire" superseded.

As you might expect in a human system, things sometimes come down to a tie. When that happens, the final BR question of the debrief is, "Do you *genuinely* believe this person raises the bar for the organization?" That's always met with silence for a moment while everyone on the loop closes their eyes to run a mental roll call, comparing the candidate to their colleagues and keeping in mind that if they hire a dud, everyone around will ask, "Who the heck was on *that* new hire's loop?" It is a self-policed mechanism.

Naturally, as time goes on, raising the bar within a massive organization becomes more difficult. To find a real-life facsimile, I investigated the most literal "bar-raising" thing I could find to see if a point could be proven. The results surprised me. According to the International Association of Athletics Federations (IAAF), the men's pole vault world record has been set 79 times in the 106 years since the IAAF started tracking it, yet it's only been raised once in the past

24 years at the time of this writing. For the ladies, it's been set 54 times in the 26 years since recording began, but the record has only been broken once in the last 9 years. That means that the last 22 percent of the years the men's record has been around—and 36 percent of the women's—the record was only broken once, as opposed to 13 new world records in the first 25 years of the men's competition and a whopping 36 for the first 9 years of the women's. Clearly, it's pretty difficult to continually raise the bar. The same ostensibly goes for companies who hire this way.

However, if we apply the "Better Than 50 Percent" rule to the current world-record pole vault heights in each of the men's and women's competitions—and therefore find half the distance between the first world record and the most recent one—you'll see something interesting and, on the surface, contradictory. There are many more world records *above* the average world-record height than below it. For the men, 25 vaults are below the 50 percent mark, while 54 jumps are above; for the women, 21 vaults are below the halfway height and 33 are above. While I'm sure pole technology has something to do with it, these data actually tell us that the higher one person raises the bar, performance improves for the system as a whole.

Finally, bar-raising sends two messages to those who are already Amazonians: first, every loop is your chance to raise the company's standards; second, you've got to keep bringing your A Game or prepare to land on a performance improvement plan someday. Essentially, if you're at Amazon long enough, you're guaranteed to be surrounded by people who should now be better than you. It serves as an organic upgrading mechanism for the future and an everyday performance incentive to existing employees all in one.

LPs IN ACTION

Now that you understand the LPs and just how important they are to the company and its approach to new talent, let's see how they're put into action through goals and programs. Before we do, however, just a small caveat: Amazon is a company of well more than half a million employees spread across multiple divisions and subsidiaries, each comprised of various orgs, with facilities and offices of all sorts in many countries and cultures. What I'm about to detail is based on—as far as I could see within Amazon Advertising and our partner orgs—the methods and techniques by which the company operates. Despite my domestic and international experience, I am not so naive as to believe this is universal within such a sprawling global enterprise. The experience conveyed herein is purely my own. Disclaimer over.

In my first one-on-one with my manager ("1:1s" are a weekly occurrence), I was told that, for most people, the first six months would be a whirlwind and that I'd be drinking from the proverbial firehose. (Boy was he right.) He also told me that this was normal and it was okay to feel as such.

"Just stay humble, listen, take notes on everything you encounter, give succinct answers, and ask questions. Asking questions when you're new does not make you look stupid here. It makes you look smart. You were hired to be inquisitive," he said. "We do not behave like any company in the world—and certainly like no agency ever has or will—so the only way to understand our peculiarities is to ask. Just know that everyone had to do the same when they started, so you're surrounded by people willing to help you. Trust me. Then, when I feel you're ready, I'll assign you your first five goals."

When football players leave college for the pros, they talk about the transition in terms of speed of play, and how it takes them months for "the game to slow down." That's exactly how I felt. My work life's change of pace from agency to Amazon can't be described without sounding hyperbolic, so I'll just leave it at that. Thankfully, things did slow down half a year in. Then, the goals assigned to me spanned five categories, one objective for each: innovation, quality, efficiency, revenue, and community. They followed the SMART Goals methodology: Specific, Measurable, Attainable, Relevant, and Time-based, and the status for each would be discussed in every 1:1 along with other business priorities, performance metrics, and departmental needs. With each passing year, one or two would be added so that, by the time I stepped down, I had 13 goals.

Even though this was some time ago, I will avoid sharing an actual goal with you (hi there, Amazon Legal) in lieu of a fictitious objective in the SMART format: "Efficiency: By September 30, build one net-new self-serve design tool that raises ADX-NY campaign output by X percent." In my time, I never saw goals sunsetted but rather revised upon their fulfillment into some new action in the same category. One's mid-term and annual performance reviews—thus promotions and stock grants—depended not only on achieving them but the quality of the data generated around tracking their progress. We were told to assume that any leader in the company—yes, even Jeff B.—should be able to ask about your goals, and the data should be readily available, demonstrable, and "clean."

Remember the smartphone analogy and how LPs represented the operating system and goals were the apps? In between the two sit the features and functions of this metaphorical Amazon device: programs. Just like goals, programs never die while you own them, they just evolve. However, *unlike* goals, programs are owned by managers (and extremely rarely individual contributors), require the owner to recruit a team to work on them, and are handed over to another manager when the owner either leaves the company or transitions to another org. Program teams can include people under one's own management, on partner teams, and even from other orgs. Whatever it takes, just get the best people on it because the clock is ticking.

Furthermore, a program is a department initiative with a long runway—something that could take a year to accomplish—and is usually borne of an org's two annual operational planning seasons, known as "OP1" and "OP2." This is when leadership gathers to exhaustively deliberate every contingency of the upcoming year, (i.e., where to invest and innovate, challenges to address, and priorities to pivot toward and away from.) They revise OP1 during OP2 season with learnings gathered during the preceding six months. These documents matriculate all the way up to the "Steam" (pronounced "S-team" despite its lack of hyphen) and the CEO himself. And it's all backed up by data from every source you can get your hands on, like operational and nonsensitive first-party customer data, and even concurrent goal and program status metrics. Here's another fake statement, this time for a program: "Drive innovation on the mobile app to increase advertiser adoption by X percent by end of Q3."

Programs are the heart and soul of what I call Amazon's "always-on innovation cycle." They are—here's that word again—relentless, and if you own one or more, you've got to demonstrate real effort toward the Bias for Action LP to assemble and motivate a team of Amazonians who already have a litany of their own goals and almost certainly other programs to handle. With time being a precious commodity, programs force you to do what I've termed "Innovate, Iterate, Automate." You're looking hard for answers and, at the same time, building a scaling solution that will not require human hands one day. I had five programs when I left the company, and they live on today. Some have already been automated.

It's important to note that goals and programs are not in addition to your day job, they *are* your day job—along with all custodial responsibilities mentioned in the role description you applied to. Now, when people wonder aloud, "How does Amazon do it?" you have the answer. With all of that nonstop stretching to innovate, down to the individual, it stands to reason that you end up with a company like this, which advances in so many "seemingly unrelated" areas of business. All year long, hundreds of thousands of Amazonians are challenged to find opportunities to better serve the customer, to look under every rock they can find to reveal a chance to surprise and delight customers because performance review time is just around the corner and they've got a body of proof to build. And it's all data-driven, which as you can guess is as prevalent as oxygen.

It's cool that as you work on fulfilling your goals and satisfying your program responsibilities, you are perfectly encouraged to make mistakes, so long as you can do two things: (1) provide evidence that you were innovating on behalf of the customer and (2) share your error with everyone on the team, your management, and the company via means like the internal wiki system so no one wastes his or her own valuable time making the same mistake somewhere else. I nicknamed this "celebrate the failure," and I came to holding "epic fail hours" for the team, during which we'd sit around a table and laugh at the stuff we did wrong with beers at week's end. This communicates that failure is valuable and the only way to innovate while sharing out the root cause, which adheres to requirement number two of the mistake code.

According to Danish physicist Niels Bohr, "An expert is a man who has made all the mistakes which can be made, in a narrow field." Bezos has a name for it: "two-way doors." If you find a two-way door—a chance to make an improvement that doesn't put the enterprise at risk, comes from the right place on behalf of the customer, and stands to generate valuable data for the company—run through it with all your might. Just do it fast and, if it doesn't work, run right back through the door and tell everyone about it. That speaks to the currency of time as, again, you cannot operate rapidly for the customer if you aren't doing it on the inside. Truth be told, all of the programs I worked on or just watched from the sidelines corresponded to at least one of the currencies, and usually more than one. I find it hardly a coincidence.

WHAT'S IT ALL MEAN TO YOU?

Amazon's operating principles and management approach

aren't right for every organization. Chances are, your company isn't ready to implement them tomorrow. But that doesn't mean you can't start with your own team. If you're a manager, lead with one voluntary program for your group. When team members raise their hand, they must understand they can't leave the program as long as they work for you. If you're an individual contributor, look at a known challenge your group routinely faces and proactively offer to start a customer-centric program of your own. Capture data the entire way and report on it frequently, whether or not you have weekly 1:1s. Then stand back and watch as the concept spreads like wildfire when others see the trappings (and attention) of success. Demonstrate Bias for Action, look for two-way doors, celebrate the failures, and move swiftly. Anyone can do it.

Amazon's culture of customer obsession is set in stone. Can you become a contagion of this ethos? Of course. Amazon doesn't own the notion of customer obsession any more than it does leadership principles or e-commerce itself. Rather, it's forcing companies that obsess over the bottom line and industry awards (or worse, shareholders) to learn customer is king and queen or pay the price. No matter what you think of this peculiar company—if you see it as a corporate phenomenon, Borg, or metaphorical smartphone—it has many effective and proven lessons to apply to your own business pursuits. Real success is out there, and the very fact that you're reading this book speaks to your penchant for advantage. This is no longer the "World Wide Wait," as Amazon comically mentioned in its original '97 letter to shareholders. The one currency we're all forced to spend every moment is running. Now is the time.

___

CHAPTER 3

Brands in the New Techonomy

"Today's corporate leaders have all the right answers. It's the questions they get wrong."

—UNCLE MILT

The air was blazing and heavy by late morning. The man's soaked dhoti clung tightly to his arms and back as he carried baskets packed with metalware from the dock to baked-earth brick storage units up the hill. His beard dripped sweat down his chest and onto his cargo. He lived up the Sabarmati River, farther away from the Arabian Sea, the source of Lothal's commercial success as a transit and distribution hub. Like most men of this small but prosperous town, he was an expert at opening, checking, repacking, and sorting containers of goods on their way to and from the major population centers of the Indus Valley and Mesopotamia during the Early Bronze Age IV: 2,200 BCE–2,000 BCE.

It would be another two millennia before the birth of Christ a thousand miles away in Palestine, but brand differentiation had already begun in what is today Saragwala, Gujarat Province, India. On the baskets, jars, and sacks containing beads, gemstones, ivory, chisels, fishhooks, bronze celts, spears, ornaments, and sundry other goods were affixed square metal seals. Onto these badges were stamped roaring tigers, rearing bulls, elephants, rhinoceros, water buffalo, and deer, as well as distinctive depictions of yogis and gods.

The containers were arranged to be redistributed quickly, so these markings were critical to their swift identification and accurate redirection. Some experts believe the seals had a secondary purpose: to promote the products inside to prospective buyers. One seal discovered featured the god of fertility, Shiva. Alas, even ancient civilizations were not immune to "sex sells."

In his book *A New History of India*, UCLA Indianologist Stanley Wolpert tells us that the seals were "probably made for merchants who used them to 'brand' their wares" alongside writing in an as yet untranslated language. They are in fact India's earliest-known business documents, and reveal an extremely advanced commerce system where differentiation was key to efficiency.

WHAT IS A BRAND, ANYWAY?

I always begin my answer to this question with what a brand is not. Contrary to how it's often used in business, a brand is not a logo or a TV campaign, nor is it a name, tagline, or marketplace positioning. Rather, a brand is a story written mentally by the customer at every touchpoint. That's every interaction, both physical and psychological. It is not an image cooked up by a marketing department or an ad agency. If the latter description fits where you work, you've probably come to understand by now that you possess little to no control over the story inside the customer's mind. Your brand is therefore not one entity but millions, depending on the widespread experiences it's generated among audience members. What *is* under your jurisdiction, however, is the identification of your core values and adherence to them in every behavior and communication in the hopes that they resonate with and are retained by the customer. That's all you got.

Indeed, the company behind a brand is also sanctioned fiction, a shared myth, a fabrication to which we all agree. As evidence, when a corporation, say, Mattress Firm files for bankruptcy as it did in October 2018, its personnel nevertheless somehow remain alive, its buildings miraculously stay upright, its debts are still marked due. How is this? That's because a corporation is an ethereal contradiction. Derived from the Latin *corpus* or "body," a corporation is actually a *disembodied* spirit that we all agree exists even though, like a religious deity, we can neither see nor touch it yet still believe in its existence.

Stories, in fact, were key to our species' dominance over this planet. In a fistfight between a burly Neanderthal and a comparatively slight *Homo sapiens*, homeboy would almost certainly get his butt kicked. But in larger groups, the table turns decidedly in favor of *sapiens*. Collective imagination of a common god or belief in a supernatural king—along with superior communication—made the better-organized and motivated *sapiens* a lock for victory. The stories we tell each other imbue us with outsized power and near-limitless potential.

Furthermore, our brand stories are often written subconsciously, deep in the recesses of the most primitive part of our brains, the limbic system, where the is jury is binary. It's fight or flight, yes or no. I think back to my last day of sixth grade—quite possibly the greatest day in the history of the world (until the next year)—when our teachers handed out ice-cold cans of Coke to the class. While I now suspect it, the 11-year-old me in his Toughskins didn't know, ask, or care whether the Coca-Cola Company was behind the experience that hot afternoon. Is it mere coincidence that I've never, ever purchased a can of Pepsi? Soda brand preference may have been hard-coded into my young cerebral cortex that day with a story written in pure, carbonated euphoria.

Okay, so a brand is a story. A cursory search of Etymonline.com reveals that "brand" evolved from the "Old English *brand, brond* 'fire, flame, destruction by fire; firebrand, piece of burning wood, torch,' and (poetic) 'sword,' from Proto-Germanic *brandaz* 'a burning.'... The definition 'mark made by a hot iron' (1550s), especially on a cask, etc., to identify the maker or quality of its contents, broadened by 1827 to marks made in other ways, then to 'a particular make of goods' (1854). *Brand-name* is from 1889; *brand-loyalty* from 1961." Indeed, we've been marking things for identification for a long time—as long ago as 2,700 BCE it is estimated, when the practice of burning figures onto livestock to declare ownership began in Egypt.

In modern terms, branding as a business got serious with the advent of the Industrial Revolution in 18th-century Manchester, England. Along with the coal dust and steam-powered looms came a new need to differentiate mass-produced goods and their manufacturers from one another. For the first time, product parity (sameness) was achievable at scale. That was great news for the technocrats of the day but resulted in a lack of distinction between competitors and confusion among customers. Furthermore, thousands of rural dwellers moved to cities for factory jobs and, in doing so, were exposed to more and more sophisticated brand messaging when considering the soap they could now purchase instead of having to make themselves on the family farm.

One of the first mentions of brand as a subject for psychological study appeared in H. D. Wolfe's 1942 article "Techniques of Appraising Brand Preference and Brand Consciousness by Consumer Interviewing." In Volume 6, Issue 4 of the *Journal of Marketing*, Wolfe, of Kent State University, laments the industry's lack of ability to attribute brand recall to conversion: "The amount of exploratory work to determine the relationship between recognition and sales has been slight."

After World War II, the consumer product bonanza kicked off in the United States as the rest of the world dug itself out of the rubble. Consumer categories of every stripe teemed with hundreds of new products competing for their share of postwar-boom wealth. According to *Advertising Age*, the number of ad agencies in the US grew from 1,628 in 1939 to 5,986 in 1948, during which time the first mass-produced electronic television set, the RCA 630-TS, would hit the shelves in 1946. With wartime advances in technology, the reduction in cost as manufacturing bloomed, and increased audience leisure time and discretionary income, brands and technology would forever walk hand in hand.

For the few thousand years leading up to today's techonomy, branding moved from the purely transactional, (i.e., information about a product's origin), to the transformational, starting with the assignment of human personality traits upon inanimate objects and, ultimately, arriving at the conveyance of a social status (hip, sexy, wealthy) upon the product's owner.

After the internet proliferation of the late '90s and the mobile revolution of 2007, marketers have been relegated to noise status. Their ads get in the way of our cat videos just as the consumer has more choice of where to spend and earn her money, information, loyalty, and time than at any point in history. The only way to succeed is to thoroughly comprehend, genuinely foster, and strive every day to increase the customer's four currencies, not your own. That will come in time if you think long term.

Now let's start with money, the most popular currency.

PART II

—

Money

CHAPTER 4

Beans

"People invented money, which unlike people, enjoys acceptance in all its forms."

—UNCLE MILT

The young man was awakened gently at dawn. His chest, smooth and brown in the early light, moved faster as he exited slumber and realized that today was the day he and his owner had long awaited. Neither said a word as the older man, a wealthy merchant, placed an elaborate feather headdress on the teenager's head and turned to leave the room. It was a cool morning in Toxcatl—the Aztec month from April 23 to May 12 on the Gregorian calendar—and it was time.

The teenager was Texlacan, and he'd been captured by the Aztecs in battle months before. Today, however, he would be the center of attention across Tenochtitlán, the site of modern-day Mexico City, where he was fed and washed not as a prisoner of war but more akin to a local celebrity. When the priests summoned, he would be clad in ceremonial dress and walked by his owner calmly through a crowd numbering in the thousands to the foot of the Great Pyramid of Tenochtitlán. Among priests and townspeople piercing and bleeding themselves to feed Huitzilopochtli, the supreme god of the Mexica whom they identified with warfare and the sun at its zenith, he would be stripped to a loin cloth and escorted up the steep face of the massive temple.

At the top, four priests guided him to a stone altar and lay him down, spreading and holding his limbs. A fifth priest produced a giant obsidian knife, raised it, and plunged it deep into the victim's chest, pulling it toward him slowly, slicing the abdomen and diaphragm as the young prisoner shrieked in agony. The high priest then carefully reached beneath the boy's ribcage to locate his heart, which the Aztecs believed to be a remnant of the sun's heat, before tearing it out, raising it to the sky in honor of the sun god, and placing it into a bowl next to the deity's statuette. The organ would beat for another four minutes. The priests would then throw the lifeless corpse down the side of the pyramid, where it would land on flower petals among the throngs of onlookers, dancers, and musicians. His body would then be taken back to the merchant's home to be cooked by the women and served at one final gala. It would be inappropriate for the merchant to eat the meat, as that would have been analogous to a father eating his son; thus, the human fare was left to the guests as he looked upon.

THE CURRENCY CONCEPT

In 15th-century Mesoamerica, affluent merchants could put their fortunes on display in front of their village by sponsoring a human sacrifice. After buying his prisoner, the merchant would shelter, feed, and clothe him in lavish style over many months at great cost ahead of the ceremony. To host the sacrifice, the merchant had to throw four banquets for fellow merchants and local military leaders, with gifts of jewelry, costume, food, and drink for all in attendance.

And he paid for it primarily with cacao seeds, the common currency. With these beans, one could purchase tomatoes, corn, jade, gold, and, yes, sacrificial victims. Plus, if one in possession of the cacao had a hankering for something sweet, he could grind his currency into a paste and mix it with water for a delicious drink. Unlike paper or metal cash—which can't be eaten and thus bear *assigned* value—chocolate beans have intrinsic value. This commodity currency was a means of exchange, but only for those who knew how to leverage its essential properties. European pirates weren't among them. When they once seized a ship carrying bales of cacao seeds, they mistook the loot for rabbit droppings and threw it overboard. So much for Itzcoatl's retirement savings.

For thousands of years, humans have demonstrated an innate need to generate and measure worth, and the Aztecs weren't alone in their adoption of commodity money. The Romans paid their soldiers in salt (the Latin word for "salt," *sal*, is the root of *salary*), early peoples throughout Oceania traded cowry shells, Mongolians exchanged bricks of tea, and Norwegians of antiquity bought with butter. Similarly, Siberians used reindeer, ancient Hittites measured value in sheep, the Greeks traded oxen, and civilizations from Ireland to North Africa used cattle to pay for everything from marriage dowries to adultery fines. (It should come as no surprise that "cattle" and "capital" share the same Latin root, *caput*, or "head.") Native Americans exchanged tobacco, and not too long after, deer skins were used to buy food, clothing, and tools by North American pioneers, and we Americans still use the word "buck" as a euphemism for "dollar" because of it.

Even people have served as currency. Vikings traded Irish slave girls in the Mediterranean, where blonde- and red-headed women were especially valued. However, of all forms of commodity money, humans were an inherently unstable currency due to their mortality rate, illness, and penchant for escaping.

THE TROUBLE WITH COMMODITY MONEY

The downside to this type of currency was that it had a shelf life. Cacao seeds can be eaten by mice, tobacco gets stale, butter melts. Cows can break a leg and die in the night as easily as wolves can devour your sheep. Furthermore, storing and feeding live animals as commodity money came at its own price. The cost of all that grain a wealthy Siberian fed his reindeer could be considered the first account management fee. In any case, all of these reasons made it virtually impossible to stockpile wealth.

Another shortcoming of commodity money was its lack of standardization. Scandinavian salted cod was prized in Southern Europe after Pope Nicholas I forbade Catholics from eating meat on Fridays in the 9th century, but it wouldn't have gotten the time of day in Indonesia.

Then a breakthrough. The first coins came into use in Lydia, an Iron Age kingdom in western Asia Minor, in what is today Turkey, around 600 BCE. These coins were made of an alloy of gold and silver called electrum and stamped with a lion's head and sunburst, King Alyattes's symbol. According to Greek historian Herodotus, the Lydians weren't just the first to mint coins but also to establish shops in permanent locations. The currency was called a "stater." A full stater has never been discovered, but fractional denominations were cut in lion head thirds, sixths, and twelfths all the way down to 1/96th amounts, along with lion paw fractions—no doubt used to finance the construction of the Temple of Artemis, one of the Seven Wonders of the Ancient World, erected by the king's son Croesus. Soon after, the first coins used for trade on a large-scale basis were likely small silver fractions, Hemiobol, minted by the Ionian Greeks in the late 6th century BCE.

How is it possible that Lydia, the birthplace of the medium so central to everything we do today is lost to history? Call it affluence-fueled arrogance. When Croesus assumed the throne, he consulted an oracle to determine if he should attack Persia. The mystic responded, "If you do, a great civilization will fall." He mistook that to mean Persia. The powerful Persian army quickly crushed the Lydians and laid waste to its capital, all but erasing the tiny kingdom from the map and primal lore—except for the mercantile system it developed, which immediately expanded throughout the Mediterranean, and Greece in particular. This new means of exchange collided with all the surrounding tributary systems (meaning: paying tribute to aristocracy for the right to live and work on their land) in existence throughout Europe and came to represent the clash between old (inherited, autocratic) and new (earned, democratic) systems of wealth generation and power. In doing so, it deteriorated kinship-based societies which relied on face-to-face interaction and shared bloodlines, accelerated community-building through a standardized value exchange, and bound disparate communities that otherwise had no language, gods, or values in common. Experts note that the spread of the money currency and resulting trade routes coincided with and even hastened the spread of a new religion: Christianity.

Thus, it was money that became the first social network, through its simplicity for acquiring something as practical as a milk cow or as abstract as work (and thus skill, strength, and time itself). The value of a work of art, musical performance, or sex act could now be quantified as easily as an apple or goat. Instead of a feudal lord charging peasants a firstborn calf or a measure of their harvest, he simply levied a tax. Religion followed suit. Gods no longer wanted a sacrifice from their worshippers. They (or more accurately, the high priest) simply commanded a tithe. The notion of civil justice did away with "an eye for an eye and tooth for a tooth," torture, and death in favor of fines.

In nearby Athens, the statesman, lawmaker, and poet Solon pursued legislation against the moral decline of ancient Greece and radically revolutionized the concept of government forever by replacing nobility as the core criterion for public office with landed wealth. It was money that single-handedly displaced aristocracy and gave rise to democracy. Prior to the commercial society that was perfected in Greece, every civilization came to power through population size and brute force. The prosperity generated in Athens bore an elite class who could now spend its ample spare time devising and perfecting the science, mathematics, technology, civics, language, history, art, education, construction, agriculture, and philosophy that are the underpinnings of everything we know today. The presence of minted coins immediately and irreversibly altered every single facet of human life by establishing a universally common denominator. It is the most obvious of the four currencies, sure, but the enormity and eponymy of its ramifications cannot be overstated. It is the single most important framework by which humanity has been organized and its progress evaluated.

MONEY AND INFLUENCE

In fact, money impacted the very structure of towns. After its arrival, municipal development saw urban footprints developed around central plazas where markets were held instead of the local palace. Trade between cultures now took place so rapidly that cartography quickly developed, and the most efficient roads and shipping lanes between cities and ports were codified to encourage even more commerce.

The fall of Rome in AD 476—due to money mismanagement of its immense military and government—sank Europe into the Dark Ages, where the money economy would not be seen in earnest again until the Knights Templar during the Crusades.

The earliest known paper currency was issued in China during the Song dynasty in the 11th century, based on merchant receipts of deposit pioneered a few hundred years earlier during the Tang. The Chinese had already been striking copper coins for centuries by this time, which featured holes in the middle so people could carry them around on ropes until, as you might imagine, they got too heavy for larger transactions. As a result, by AD 960, the central government began issuing notes called *jiaozi* which could be used alongside the tokens.

Bills of exchange were introduced to the West by the banking families of Northern Italy exploiting a loophole in Christian dogma which outlawed usury, or charging a tax on loaned money. The word "bank" is derived from the Italian *banco*, meaning "bench," upon which these families' representatives would discuss financial matters with people at countryside fairs. These bills both relieved money of its physical limitations as well as prevented currency shortages in whichever country they were signed. Furthermore, the paper bills unshackled money from its reliance on the amount of gold or silver available in the area and could be written in any one of dozens of currencies and then cashed out in another somewhere else.

Italian bankers thrived until the entire region was ravaged by the Black Death, but their principles were too sensible not to live on. When the area finally overcame the plague in the 1400s, these families sought the same enviable status in the community and high posts in the church as the nobility to whom they leant money and whose fortunes they protected. So they went on terrific spending sprees of palazzos, art, and monstrous urban dwellings and, in doing so, just happened to ignite the Renaissance in Florence.

While relatively late to the game, the Medici family is today synonymous with the earliest formalized, international banking centers and accompanying fortunes. Their bank operated until Charles VIII of France invaded Florence in 1494, collapsed that republic, and took all of its holdings back with his army to the coffers of Paris. The die had been cast, however. By strategically marrying, as well as already holding lofty positions in every aspect of government, church, and what we call today the "private sector" across Europe, the Medici had become the most powerful family of their time. Together with the other wealthy families of Florence, they had prioritized education—specifically math, which was mandatory to calculating profit and loss, computing interest rates, and speculating—so much so that the Renaissance began not as an art movement but more an emphasis on the fundamentals of numbers and letters. This also resulted in the dismissal of clumsy Roman numerals and the abacus in favor of Arabic numbers, a stylus, and paper, facilitating the abstract concepts of multiplication, percentages, and fractions for the average person without higher education. In 1439, Johannes Gutenberg's new printing press assured the proliferation of mathematics. Indeed it was here where the money economy forever changed how commoners evaluate and convey the world to one another.

Following Christopher Columbus's Caribbean arrival in 1492, the Spanish Empire would rule most of the Americas for three centuries after Hernán Cortés's conquistadors built a pipeline sending untold sums of gold and silver back to

King Ferdinand and Queen Isabella. The fortune generated by this golden age was unprecedented in the history of the world, and those bottomless American mines financed Spanish empirical efforts throughout Europe and North Africa. Its power appeared unrivalled until it ran out of cash after overspending on conquest and getting punched in the nose by the Dutch, English, French, and Portuguese.

Around the time Columbus sailed the ocean blue, rich silver deposits were discovered in the Krušnè Hory ("Cruel Mountains") in the Kingdom of Bohemia, modern-day Czech Republic. In 1518, a local count by the name of Stephan Schlick took over the burgeoning mining camp and christened it St. Joachimsthal, or "St. Joachim's Valley," to honor the father of the Virgin Mary and lend a bit of class to the ramshackle place. That year, he instructed his metallurgists to start minting silver coins from the cellars of his massive stone castle. His ingots were larger and heavier than any other currency, and because the valley's mines were so bountiful, the metal disks were struck at a prodigious rate, hastening their adoption and popularity as far away as England and Spain. Once in heavy circulation, they were nicknamed in German "Joachimsthalers." Four syllables were apparently too many, even for the Germans, so the name soon shortened to the more convenient "thaler," which in English was pronounced "dollar."

"Dollar" entered the English language by way of Scotland,

whose citizens used the term to delineate themselves from their domineering southern neighbor and its monetary unit, the English Pound Sterling. Thus, from its earliest days, the dollar carried a sort of anti-English tinge to it, and when Scots emigrated by the thousands to colonies in North America during the 1600s, they carried the word with them. When the Bank of England forbade the export of the pound—even to its own foreign outposts—it forced American colonists to use silver coins from other countries, especially Mexico, which operated one of the world's largest mints. A member state of the Spanish Empire, Mexico stamped *pesos de ocho*, or "pieces of eight," upon these denominations worth eight Spanish *reales*, and circulated them throughout the Americas. The US dollar and Mexican peso are so intertwined through history that the quarter was known as "two bits," and many believe the "$" sign was inspired by the two pillars of Hercules and S-shaped banners on the peso's reverse side. In fact, the Mexican peso enjoyed legal tender status throughout the United States until Congress passed the Coinage Act of 1857.

On the eve of the American Civil War in 1861, there were suddenly two sets of notes on the American landscape: the United States of America dollar and the Confederate States of America (CSA) dollar, dubbed the "greyback." Interestingly, the Citizens Bank of Louisiana printed CSA ten-dollar bills with the French word for ten, *dix*, on one side to accommodate its Creole population. The note came to be known as the "dixie," and the South, "the land of Dixie."

In wartime, nations are often forced to make radical, sometimes history-altering choices, as when US Secretary of the Treasury Salmon P. Chase underestimated the Civil War in terms of duration and cost. Running out of money to pay Union soldiers, President Abraham Lincoln and his government faced a tough decision: print its own money (theretofore, the only US currency had been silver and gold coins) or go deep into debt with foreign lenders. He chose the former, and in July of that year, Congress ratified the issue of $50 million in Demand Notes backed only by the credibility of the US government, not gold or silver. This amount ultimately proved insufficient, so a year later, Congress authorized the printing of $150 million more "greenbacks," this time as notes which could be redeemed for goods and services.

This move would be emulated by Britain 57 years later to finance its World War I efforts, alongside increasing its tax base (in 1913, only 2 percent of the population paid income tax; 2.4 million people would be added during the war), borrowing from its own citizens in the form of war bonds, and taking loans from other countries. It nearly bankrupted the UK, but Dear Ol' Blighty is still standing, so the greater good was served. However, it would not be until March 2015 before it settled its outstanding debts from the first big one.

I detail its long and fascinating history because money, like necessity in times of duress, is a mother of invention. The malleable nature of perceived value depends solely on those assigning it and their respective states of need. As we've moved through the generations, the concept of worth has been distorted to suit the situation of its participants. In today's actual monetary value, it costs the US Bureau of Engraving and Printing 12.5 cents to print a $100 bill, so the remaining $99.875 of worth is fabricated, made up, *assigned*. We all agree it's worth a hundred, so, snap, it's worth a cool hundred.

Since the first minted coins back in Lydia, gold had remained the highest standard of all physical currencies. Because it never tarnishes or oxidizes, gold is chemically the least likely to corrode and, therefore, lose value. Plus, like the Aztecs' cacao seeds, the material can be used in multiple ways (jewelry, decoration, electrical conduction). Some have ascribed a deeper meaning to its fixation by ancient cultures, as its luster resembles the sun and thus may have held religious or supernatural sentiment. Again, the value of gold is timeless but no less imaginary. It relies wholly on trust between two parties that the terms of the transaction won't change. Since gold doesn't change over time, it serves as a shiny metaphor for the constancy of a value exchange. (This is another reason why loyalty, a stand-in for trust, is one of the four brand currencies.)

In 1971, the "Nixon Shock" took place when President Richard Nixon yanked the US dollar off the gold standard and replaced its backing with the reputation of the United States. The rest of the world's trust in the stability of the country, he believed, was enough. In 1996, Paul Krugman—who went on to win the Nobel Memorial Prize in Economic Sciences in 2008—summed up the move as such: "The current world monetary system assigns no special role to gold; indeed, the Federal Reserve is not obliged to tie the dollar to anything. It can print as much or as little money as it deems appropriate. There are powerful advantages to such an unconstrained system. Above all, the Fed is free to respond to actual or threatened recessions by pumping in money. To take only one example, that flexibility is the reason the stock market crash of 1987—which started out every bit as frightening as that of 1929—did not cause a slump in the real economy."

What is credit then but money multiplied by time and the assurance you'll pay? With his "shock," Nixon simply said, "We're good for it," to the rest of the world, and for the most part, it's worked. The issuer of a credit instrument simply sells time at a specified (interest) rate. The longer you take to pay, the more you'll have to shell out to settle up. In the end though, it's all just an agreement. If one party breaks the agreement, his reputation is harmed, which will make it more difficult to receive credit later. Trust is money.

This is how food stamps, airline miles, Linden dollars from virtual world *Second Life*, and many other forms of quasi-currency work. It's also why the share price of a company's stock plummets when its CMO is caught cooking the books. Human beings expect promises to be upheld, and a promise—the *real* value of the transaction—can take any physical or metaphysical form we want. Or none at all. Take foreign exchange (FX) trading for instance, considered the purest market of them all. The relationship between any two currencies is in constant flux due to factors like their respective nations' debt, interest and inflation rates, and government stability. Basically, speculators are using a mathematical crystal ball to determine the future "reputation" of an economy before buying or selling its currency. CLS, a leading settler of FX market exchanges, calculated the average daily traded volume at $1.87 trillion between January and March 2018. You read correctly—*daily*. Quite the reputation analysis.

IN MONEY WE TRUST

Money is thus a psychological phenomenon, a most human expression of trust in itself. But when it comes to corporate revenue and expenditure, it seems to skew brand owners' perception into believing it to be the end-all be-all. I call this syndrome "Please the Shareholders" or "PTS." Yes, money is a language all cultures speak, but when it's the first thing you think about when making decisions, you're on the road to failure as a company and brand. As we've learned, we can assign value to anything we want, so get rid of PTS *tout de suite* and replace it with "Please the Customer."

As mentioned in the previous chapter, one of Amazon's LPs is Frugality. It's applied everywhere—not just in terms of money but also time. Email hygiene and meeting conduct, including purposeful and succinct agendas, contribute as much to frugality as not providing free lunch in its office cafeterias and demanding all employees print double-sided in black and white. The customer's money is the engine at the back of any company's information, loyalty, and time locomotive, and minimizing operational expenditure directly translates to lower prices for her. Bezos has been quoted as saying, "High-profit margins justified rivals' investments in R&D and attracted more competition, while low margins attracted more customers and were more defensible." In short, it pays to remain patient, charge as little as you can afford, and focus on long-term customer trust instead of short-term profit.

Money is arguably the most fantastically successful of man's inventions. It provided first a tangible and later intangible vehicle within which the best and worst human impulses could travel. From 85 to 43 BCE, Publilius Syrus was a Syrian slave who was brought to Italy and freed by his master for displaying incredible wit. All that survives of his work is *Sententia*, a collection of moral axioms and verses. One reads, "Money alone sets all the world in motion," while another claims, "A good reputation is more valuable than money." They're both true. Not long after Syrus, a Latin translation of Greek Bible manuscripts read, *Radix malorum est cupiditas*, or "Root for all the evil is the love of money." I don't see it that way. The root of all evil isn't money. It's bad parenting.

CHAPTER 5

———

Money and the Customer

"Only those who discipline their children may complain about high taxes."

—UNCLE MILT

Now let's ease our way into the currencies with money, the most popular. From here, the book will evaluate each currency on the individual level through a sort of new-world microeconomic lens. (Microeconomics concentrates on individuals like households, workers, and businesses within the economy, while macroeconomics looks at broad matters like GDP, unemployment, and inflation.)

Everything we do once we become sentient toddlers is a value exchange. What are we willing to give up in return for something else? We navigate the world looking to spend as little as possible for as much as we can get. Survival of the fittest.

And the same applies to our relationships with brands and the products and services they represent.

For each currency, we'll start (of course) with the customer spending and receiving, and then do the same for brands. Beginning with money sets up a logical context that we'll repeat for information, loyalty, and time. Now let's kick off with some learnings from legendary 18th-century Scottish economist Adam Smith.

Ours is a market economy in which households sell their labor as workers to firms in return for wages, salaries, and benefits. Decision-making is decentralized, going by the laws of supply and demand to regulate production and labor. The foundation of the market economy is private enterprise. Private citizens, or groups of them, own and operate resources and businesses. Here, a person's income is based on his or her ability to transform labor into something valued by society. The more society values the person's work, the higher his or her income. Hello Beyoncé, George Clooney, and Jeff Bezos. In this framework, market forces, not governments, drive the economy. This is pretty much the opposite of command economies—China and Cuba, for example—where the government owns the resources and businesses, and the supply of goods and services depends wholly upon what their leaders decree.

Now then, on what does our customer spend most of the money she earns? The US Bureau of Labor Statistics told us in

2017 that the average American household spends 62 percent of its money on just three things: housing, transportation, and food. From there, in descending order, come insurance/pensions, healthcare, entertainment, apparel and services, cash contributions, education, miscellaneous, personal care, alcohol, tobacco, and reading. (What could be in miscellaneous that exceeds booze, smokes, and reading?) No wonder people aren't saving for the future. Using data from the Federal Reserve and the Federal Deposit Insurance Corporation, MagnifyMoney, in a report it issued in September 2017, calculated that fewer than half of all US households have saved more than $4,830. In fact, nearly 30 percent of Americans have less than $1,000 saved.

One data point conspicuously left off the Bureau of Labor Statistics expenditure list was taxes. (I assume state and local taxes are baked into the various spending categories.) When most Americans think of federal taxes, the first thing that comes to mind is the income tax due every April 15. The personal income tax is the largest single source of US federal government revenue, and it's easy to see why. The average American pays $10,489 in "personal taxes," representing 14 percent of her household's average total income of $56,000. If taxes represented an individual line item, it would be number 2 on the list between housing ($18,409) and transportation ($9,503).

All of the above have led many Americans to borrow. Findings from an October 2018 ValuePenguin study combining data from the US Census Bureau and Federal Reserve indicate the average US household bears $5,700 in credit card debt. The average for balance-carrying families is $9,333. Worse, households with the lowest net worth (zero or negative) owe an average of $10,308 to their credit cards. In total, it adds up to $3.9 trillion in outstanding US consumer debt and a revolving debt total of $1.03 trillion.

WEALTH AND RELATIVITY

Around the world, Americans are viewed as an optimistic bunch. This was a premonition exposed by Brooklyn-born economist Milton Friedman (no relation to Uncle MILT) in his landmark 1957 book *A Theory of the Consumption Function*, earning him the 1976 Nobel Prize in Economic Sciences for research on consumption analysis. There, Friedman puts forth his permanent income hypothesis, positing that an individual's consumption at any point in time is determined not just by her current income but also by her future, expected income—in aggregate, her "permanent income." In layman's terms, from *Popeye*'s Wimpy, "I'd gladly pay you Tuesday for a hamburger today."

Attitudes one has regarding his or her own wealth are relative to be sure, but it turns out the happiness it can buy might not be. According to a 2010 study from Princeton University's Woodrow Wilson School, if you make anything more than

$75,000 a year, you feel as content as the person making exactly $75,000. No more, no less. Of course, the lower a person's annual income falls below that amount, the less happy the earner is. But according to the responses of 450,000 Americans surveyed by Healthways and Gallup in 2008 and 2009, no matter how much more than $75,000 people earned, they didn't report any greater degree of happiness.

Wealth is relative because, if you really think about it, money doesn't automatically equal good fortune. Rather, being rich is about options. Ask the guy who got busted running a Ponzi scheme, with millions socked away in Swiss bank accounts, if he feels rich while sitting in prison. He's loaded—but not with what matters most. His only option is which white-collar gang to avoid in the yard. By proxy, the real power lies in giving customers the most options with their money. This is where Amazon shines. It offers "Earth's biggest selection." Selection is gold, Jerry.

As Adam Smith informed us, customers receive money by selling their work to firms. (He omitted that one can *inherit* wealth, but that's just a time-delayed output of someone else's work or royal conquesting, itself an ancient form of employ.) As of the time of this writing, unemployment in the US is approaching half-century lows. But this is where micro- and macroeconomics diverge.

The truth is, most Americans' wages have been reduced year

over year due to stagflation—wage stagnation compounded by inflation. While Wall Street has been booming the past decade (the signs over the horizon show clearly it's all about to change at the time of this writing), a report from the Organization for Economic Cooperation and Development (OECD) shows us that policymakers have endeavored to create a system that disempowers workers in lieu of a higher share of economic growth for executives and shareholders. (*Again* with the shareholders.) In the US, nearly 15 percent of workers earn less than half the medium wage. Only Spain and Greece are lower. In terms of income inequality, which is earnings at the 90th percentile as a multiple of earnings at the 10th percentile, the US is second only to Israel. Couple those data with the fact that US workers enjoy fewer protections than most countries' and stingier benefits when out of work than all but one developed nation by share of total wealth, Slovakia, and I hope you appreciate that things are a wee bit tense for our customers.

Of course, the aforementioned boom in equities offers some customers another way to increase their discretionary income, but mathematically, it's unlikely. According to New York University economist Edward N. Wolff, the top 10 percent of American households owned 84 percent of all stocks in 2016. Perhaps more surprising is that the top 1 percent of households own around 40 percent of all stocks. That disparity continues to widen.

WHAT'S IT ALL MEAN TO YOU?

So that's what you and your brand are up against. Asking your customer to part ways with her money? Get in line behind the mortgage, Uncle Sam, transport to work, breakfast, lunch, and dinner. And you'd better be damn sure you're ready to overserve—and do it humbly—or else. This is where keeping costs low on behalf of the customer is the only reasonable approach. One-off discounts are commodities anymore. Upon checkout at almost any online shop, I can search for a promo code and, with zero effort or loyalty to the site or brand, take a few percentage points off its already-razor-thin margin. This is exactly the reason why skimping on customer service is death by one paper cut across the throat. It's not *if* you'll bleed out, but when.

It's also why perceived value has played an enormous role in the success of Amazon Prime and its little sister, Prime Now. Including more and more extras inside today's $119 annual fee has, against analysts' admonitions in 2005, made Amazon even more of a retail powerhouse. Giving and giving and giving more—from free two-day shipping, video and music streaming, access to Prime Day and other events and services, Prime Now with free two-hour delivery of millions of products in 52 US cities (at the time of this writing) and dozens more overseas, and exclusive deals and products—have made Amazon Prime the killer retail app.

Money is an extremely important currency even here in the

US, the world's wealthiest nation, for the customer. But if you think it's the most important, disavow that notion at once. The new techonomy has different ideas, which we'll get to soon. Until then, let's view money from the brand's perspective.

CHAPTER 6

Money and the Brand

"With all due respect to the Beatles, love can buy you money."

—UNCLE MILT

My knees ain't what they used to be. This became sorely apparent on 12-hour flights from London to Tokyo. Ah, coach to Asia—the only way to fly. Moments after clearing customs, my brand loyalty to Advil would activate as I spotted its familiar blue package from the concourse at Haneda Airport, and the joint swelling brought about by the Amazon LP Frugality would begin to subside.

As I established earlier, brands aren't companies. They're stories. As such, a story cannot spend or earn money. Brand owners do. So we're going to blur the lines for the sake of the framework of this book by extending "brand" to include the organization and people who manage it. People interact with brands and constantly revise the story to which they attribute them, so from the consumer's perspective, we'll refer to a brand "spending" as a company's allocation of resources, marketing and otherwise, that affect the customer experience.

Over the years, it is my experience that most brand owners spend cautiously. Like all departments within any enterprise, Marketing, Advertising, Brand Management, and the like all receive a budget from the CFO at the start of the fiscal year which grows and shrinks (usually the latter) in reaction to the successes or challenges experienced by the wider business as the year rolls on. Every dollar counts and patience is limited. According to *Forbes*, as of March 2018, the average CMO's tenure is 44 months, down from 48 months in 2014. That article also assessed their median tenure (less influenced by outliers) at just 31 months. This is due primarily to the fact that expectations of conversions per dollar spent have soared with the advent of sales attribution technologies. Not too dissimilar from head coaches in the NFL. If you don't have a winning record within a few years, you're unceremoniously sent packing.

BRANDS, SPENDS, AND SWAY

I'll dispense with payroll; fixed costs, including real estate and facilities; and things like supplier and vendor contracts. Let's focus instead on how brands spend to lean forward and influence customers—keeping in mind they can be anyone who interacts with your brand, as Amazon sees them, not just the folks buying your product or service—including employees, the press, regulators, and anyone who so much as hears your brand's name.

What do companies spend on? According to an August 2017 report from CMOSurvey.com, marketing budgets in the US range between 7 and 12 percent of total revenue, per its 349 CMO respondents. Some companies, like Amazon, do not prioritize self-promotion and decide instead to plow most of that money back into R&D budgets, preferring to market by example with more and better products. Innovation is the new marketing for these corporations who see word of mouth and social shares as much more authentic and trustworthy mechanisms to drive consumer awareness and engagement.

Right now, ad spend in America is literally at a crossroads. Per eMarketer's *US Ad Spending 2018* report from October of that year, allocation to digital media should overtake traditional media for the first time ever in 2019. During the first half of 2018, digital ad investments surpassed its March 2018 estimate of $107.30 billion and are expected to reach $111.14 billion by year's end. In 2019, according to the report, digital media will account for 55 percent of total media ad spend.

Of course, advertising is just one of many ways brands allocate resources, the collective impact of which can divert precious funds away from improving the customer experience. If a company is more interested in, say, lobbying DC lawmakers for lower corporate taxes, those millions could have gone to expanding its call centers. If a firm demonstrates poor corporate citizenship and constantly finds itself in court, the moneys required to defend itself could have been used instead on technologies to reduce prices or even shipping times. Indeed, restraint in all areas of the organization can translate directly to long-term business success if the budget withheld were instead deployed on behalf of the customer.

For its employees, Amazon is synonymous with a lot of things—data, discipline, and results chief among them. Everything is meticulously quantified so it can be reduced to its practical minimum. Meeting duration, ink and toner (we had to plead for years to gain access to a color printer), and turning off the air conditioning at 6 p.m. every weeknight are but a few. Oh, and people too. "We run lean here" is a commonly heard phrase, often followed by, "We throw intelligence, not people, at problems." The list of frugalities could go on, but you get the idea. No option escapes the spotlight to see where money could be saved in order to keep prices low for the customer. It doesn't make 12-hour flights all that fun, but after a while, you get it and learn to adapt along with everybody else.

Additionally, like all companies, Amazon has sources of incremental free cash flow, or money not used for operational expenditures (OpEx) and capital expenditures (CapEx), including Amazon Web Services and Amazon Advertising, which drive revenue outside the e-commerce business. Unlike the overwhelming majority of companies, Amazon unapologetically puts every cent it can right back into the business to reduce prices, offer more and better information, increase loyalty, and save time. For years, this approach prompted Wall Street to snidely nickname the company "Amazon.org"—with the ".org" stigmatizing it as a not-for-profit due to its record of eschewing shareholder value for growth. AMZN stockholders today are delighted with the results of minimum viable OpEx generating maximum viable CapEx, which, along with strategically timed bond sales in years past, have gone a long way toward the company's expansion into sector after sector.

Naturally, companies make money selling their products and services to individuals, other businesses, and governments. For public companies, it is often the brand which can do a lot to draw capital from investors. The stronger a company's reputation (a brand is a story), the more predisposed a person or institution will be to want to own a piece of it. Drip by drip, Amazon's ".org" became a ".com" in the eyes of the market because of rigorous operational governance and unyielding commitment to innovation. At the time of this writing, the AMZN market cap sits just north of $823 billion, well more than double than where it was two years prior.

On the other hand, brands can certainly take a hit for their economic behavior. Beyond the obvious, like embezzlement or outright fraud, a customer's mental story can be significantly altered by how brands play in the financial sandbox. People who invest their money in equities are certainly customers like anyone else, as are the employees of institutional investors who buy stock in bulk on their trading desks' dime. However, let's not be Pollyannaish. There's an elephant in the room when it comes to Amazon in this arena. The company has taken its share of flack for paying a low federal tax rate here at home and winning big-time tax breaks abroad. When the question was raised internally to leadership when I worked there, we were always assured that Amazon follows the legal provisions to a T. Nothing I learned as an employee or have read since my departure has indicated otherwise. These issues have drawn negative sentiment upon the brand, as Carrie Customer and the rest of us pay taxes through our noses.

Another touchy area where brands spend is lobbying, or the practice of influencing policymakers' votes with political donations, information, connections, and other means. Lobbying has been around for a long time, and has its origins in the halls (lobbies) of UK Parliament, where constituents would hang around and wait to appeal to their MPs after adjournment. If done by the book, lobbying is perfectly legal. As Amendment I of the US Constitution reads: "Congress shall make no law...abridging the right of the people peaceably...

to petition the Government for a redress of grievances." So technically, it should be no threat to a company's reputation, right?

The fact is, most of us individuals could never afford a lobbyist, which means the interests attended to are primarily those of the wealthiest Americans, major corporations, and special interest groups. A 2016 Gallup poll of 1,027 adults yielded 64 percent of respondents believe major donors have "a lot" of influence on legislation versus just 14 percent who believe influence rests with the voting citizens of a politician's district. Proving that Americans from both sides of the aisle can agree on something, the numbers are remarkably similar across the political spectrum. OpenSecrets.org tells us that a total of $3.37 billion was spent on lobbying in the US in 2017, with the pharmaceuticals/health products and insurance sectors leading the way at $279,884,983 and $162,453,585, respectively. The top corporate spender (i.e., nonindustry association or chamber of commerce) was Blue Cross Blue Shield, which clocked in at $24,330,306. It's naive to deem that, while legal, participating in this trade can't hurt your brand. A 2013 Gallup poll ranked members of Congress and lobbyists at the bottom of the list—below car salespeople—in terms of honesty. Are you sure that's the company you want your brand to keep?

Our government doesn't have a stellar brand in general (does any?), and the sour taste in our mouths extends to many mundane yet important issues like our health. In 2015, Reuters published a news report stating that the US consumer pays three times more than her UK counterpart for the world's 20 top-selling drugs. When I lived in London, I saw it firsthand. All the way down to Nicorette gum, everything in the pharmacy was significantly cheaper there than in the States. This lack of governmental price control just adds to Americans' collective headache, because we know the pharmaceutical industry leads in lobbying, yet our prices are still 16 times higher than Brazil's for the identical medicine. It's enough to make you sick.

There's a parallel for all brands in that paragraph. As a customer, if I'm paying a lot for something, yet prices continue to rise, however modestly, yet I experience no increase in quality or innovation, it's easy to see I'm being taken advantage of. Come on, Brand X. You know that's unfair as hell, and now you have an enemy in me and anyone else that'll listen. This is precisely what fueled the two biggest retail upheavals of the past decade.

INNOVATE, DISINTERMEDIATE

Mattresses are a $29 billion industry globally. In 2014, a scant few had heard of an online-only bed company; of those who had, most believed it would never work. In its corner, however, was the fact that for so many customers over the years, going to a mattress store felt one chromosome away from visiting a used car lot. Enter New York City–based Casper, which armed itself with a "unique combination of high-density foams" and took on the giants. They innovated, kept costs low, offered a 100-night trial with free returns, and shipped them to your house in a box. Word spread quickly, and people (and the media) noticed. *Time Magazine*, for example, named the bed one of its 25 Best Inventions of 2015, and *Fast Company* bestowed upon the Brooklynites a 2017 Most Innovative Companies honor. Casper now lays claim to being "America's #1 mattress brand" (per their website). In contrast, Sealy Corporation was founded in 1881—11 years before General Electric—and by the mid-20th century was the world's largest mattress company. How could they have been blindsided by this little hipster enterprise? How were they not listening to customers and innovating? What have they been doing with their customers' money?

Likewise, male grooming is a massive business sector, esti- mated at $21 billion worldwide. The term "safety razor" was first used in an 1847 patent application by William Henson, who described his invention as resembling "somewhat the form of a common hoe." Then Gillette came along in 1901 and Schick followed 25 years later, after which the two dom- inated the industry for generations. Fast-forward 92 years to a party where two guys got to talking about how ridiculous razor blade prices had become and how demeaning it is for men to have to ring a stupid bell to call a pharmacy worker to unlock them. So Mark Levine and Michael Dubin started

Dollar Shave Club. Five years later, the startup was acquired by Unilever for a reported $1 billion in cash. Gillette had a consumer base of millions, a global footprint, and 110 years to think of online subscription models, improved design, and high-quality products at fair prices. Instead, they spent their customer's money on other things, like $8 million a year for 15 years to name a stadium that most people still call Foxboro. (Gillette ended up launching their own Gillette On Demand service in 2017 anyway.)

What's more, there's still enough room left in their respective industries for fast followers. Casper inspired Leesa, Tuft & Needle, Purple, and more than a dozen others. Dollar Shave Club was joined by Harry's in 2013 and later entrants like Morgans and Birchbox Man. For giant, established monoliths, is it too late to innovate at the speed and agility of a startup—one that's not saddled with all the politics, lethargic and petrified legal departments, and bloated R&D cycles? Probably, but it doesn't have to be. Beats the alternative. Dollar Shave Club's Durbin delivered the commencement address to Emory University graduates in May 2018, where he focused on the importance of choices in life. Of the six choices he detailed, number three is my favorite: "Get comfortable with being uncomfortable." No one—not brand owners, not your significant other, not your boss—likes to feel uncomfortable. But I can think of few things less comfortable than going out of business. Your company will be next if you're foolish with your customer's money.

At Amazon, the self-important and slow are referred to as "Day 2" companies. "Day 1" is the two-word pledge to always remain hungry, humble, and eager to serve the customer, as if today is the first day of business. "Day 1" means you will never run out of things to learn and you must be scrappy with limited resources. You can't pay problems to solve themselves. In his 2017 letter to the shareholders—two decades after the original—Bezos implored, "Day 2 is stasis. Followed by irrelevance. Followed by excruciating, painful decline. Followed by death. And that is why it is always Day 1." A building on the Seattle campus is named Day 1, as is the company's official blog. It is everywhere during your tenure there. "That's Day 2 thinking" is the Amazonian equivalent of an expletive-laden insult. The biggest Day 2 offenders in my career experience are some of the oldest, biggest brands in the land, where employees would need to stab a colleague in the eye with a billiard cue to get fired. Thus, no one takes risks or even speaks up in those nondescript cubicle farms, where everyone does their best to remain unnoticed. Additionally, those companies' OpEx is overweight because there's negligible turnover and, thus, widespread complacency. These lifers whisper to one other, "Just wait one more year until I retire, and then you can do what you want when I'm gone. Please, I beg you, don't upset any apple carts, and if you do, don't involve me." The problem with a line of thinking so common to these corporate anachronisms is that, at any given moment, there's a never-ending conga line of senior decision-makers with one year left to retirement. No Day 2 executive wants to be the one to fail, so even mundane decisions take forever, and nothing significant ever gets done. Worst of all, to survive, these corpulent beasts must keep prices high, and it's the customer who's left with the dinner bill. Startups: commit to yourselves right now that growth will never equal morbid obesity. Amazon has more than half a million employees worldwide, and take my word for it, the last descriptors one could possibly use to describe the place are "slow" and "risk-averse."

One more thought. If you're starting a challenger brand or looking to transform into a nimbler, more customer-centric company, the answer might not just be a less-expensive product, like a slick razor design or a bed in a box, to gain market share. Take Airbnb and Uber, which have disintermediated the immense hospitality and mobility industries by thinking completely differently about something as humdrum as, well, *empty space*. Got an unused room in your house or a car sitting in your driveway? May as well make money on the cubic footage inside if someone's willing to rent it. Solutions are all around. Get comfortable searching uncomfortable places you never considered before.

I recently attended a talk at Advertising Week here in New York City by venture capitalist and cryptocurrency pioneer Bill Tai. There, he said something that struck and stuck with me that helps bring the point home (I wasn't recording, so allow me to paraphrase): *Airbnb isn't a hotel company and*

Uber isn't a transportation company. They're cloud *companies with nodes of customer value on the edges.* I thought that was spot-on, and you can learn from it: use data to find areas of unmet need and then spend the money your customer gives you precisely there. This was clearly not how the railway magnates thought of their industry in the early 1900s, causing them to miss out on a once-in-ten-lifetimes chance to own the business of air travel. Big rail had the land, logistics expertise, and certainly financial power, but it considered itself a provider of trains, not mobility, and squandered a historic opportunity to change the world.

In summary, the only money your business has is because of your customers. Yes, there's *saving* money, as in corporate tax breaks and loopholes, but when it comes to old-fashioned revenue, it was theirs until they considered, thought, thought again, and decided to give it to you in exchange for your promise. Strangely, after a while, companies somehow get arrogant. They bite the hands that feed them because they've become "outsolated," like a politician who's asked how much a carton of eggs costs and can't give an answer, proving he's nowhere near the commoner he pretends to be. Spend every possible bean you can on your customers—learning about them, listening to them, responding quickly to them, delighting them, predicting their needs, and saving them their own money, not yours. Nothing in modern business is simpler, more difficult, or more critical. Your knees might swell up in coach, but your ego sure won't.

PART III

—

Information

CHAPTER 7

Bits

"Find patterns in the work of man and nature. They are never coincidental."

—UNCLE MILT

The shadows lengthened along the Lokounje River. Dusk is a quiet time here, except for the singing bush larks and the odd chimpanzee screech from the dense forest undergrowth. The din of crickets, mosquitoes, and flies is ever-present in South Cameroon so as to render the mélange unnoticeable. At last, the sun bows behind the rich green canopy and, for the first time since morning, yields its oppression.

In the twilight, the silence is broken from a distance. *DA ba-buh da-BA BAP-buh-da BAP-buh-da.* An elderly man appears at the entrance of his hut and tilts his head toward the river. Two breaths later, the sequence is repeated. *DA ba-buh da-BA BAP-buh-da BAP-buh-da.* A woman carrying a bushel, emerging from the foliage on her return from the forest garden, stops dead in her tracks and, like the man, cants her head in the direction of the river.

The clearing amid the huts is soon populated with a dozen village elders, whispering in their native Bulu, *A nto ane jomolo jomolo*, in tones so hushed they're practically mouthing the phrase. "He is as weakening weakening." The villagers solemnly return to their homes to prepare gifts for their neighboring tribe, gathering eggs, plantains, maize, and yams for the morning procession.

At dawn, the Bulu hear a new arrangement: *Ba-ba buh BAP-a-buh BAP-a-buh BAP-a-buh BAP-buh-DA*. "Only folds folds folds hands on breast." The chief of the Bakola, five miles to the West, is dead.

No one knows how long the talking drums of Africa had been in use before the Germans claimed the territory of Kamerun in 1884. So when Westerners first heard them, they assumed the natives were simply playing music. But they'd soon learn this early wireless communications network could successfully transmit information upwards of 100 miles an hour—in orders of magnitude faster than any horseman could possibly imagine, particularly with the countryside's near-impenetrable vegetation and negligible infrastructure.

African languages are tonal, meaning that the pitch of the

speaker's voice carries meaning that distinguishes similar words from one another. The talking drum was an expertly hollowed-out hardwood log, anywhere between two and four feet long, that offered different tones depending on where it was struck. Along the top of the log were two rectangular slits of different sizes, the "man" and the "woman," separated by a section of the exterior left intact. The drumsticks were about a foot long and crafted from softer wood. When the drummer was finished sending a message, he or she would store the sticks by placing them into the drum through the slits, which made for a sort of audible end-punctuation. *BAP.*

THE MOST POWERFUL CURRENCY

We all know money is a currency. Now let's turn and apply those same principles to the sending and receiving of data. The need to exchange information for survival is as old as the brain stem, which is why I believe it deserves currency status—not only that, but I'm convinced that information is the most powerful of the brand currencies. It's been said that one pair of walkie-talkies would've been way more effective than a machine gun at quickly ending the Civil War. I concur. Put simply, if you have the right information, you can do much more for your customer than without to save her money and time and drive her loyalty. As for money, what is a winning lottery ticket than a mere set of numbers at the right time? Forgive the obtuse example, but if you possess that information before the drawing, you're rich. To my mind, information is the howitzer of currencies.

Like a brand, history is a nonfictional account, complete with the beholder's biases implicit. It is the story of information becoming self-aware, starting with the advent of written language, before which nothing could be recorded aside from one's memory. In an oral culture, the idea of looking something up simply did not exist. That changed in ancient Egypt, where hieroglyphs are believed to have been developed sometime around 3,200 BCE and would remain in use until the Middle Bronze Age, when Proto-Sinaitic script arose between the mid-19th and mid-16th centuries BCE. That was the first known alphabet—the name bestowed upon the system by the Phoenicians by joining the first two of its 22 characters, alpha and beta. It spread like a virus.

Writing things down was not without its critics. In an argument not too dissimilar from the modern-day "the internet has made us dumb," Socrates resists the technology as a destroyer of memory in Plato's *The Phaedrus*. In the dialogue, Socrates reprises the story of the god Theuth, who offers King Thamus the gift of letters to share with his people:

> "This, said Theuth, will make the Egyptians wiser and give them better memories; it is a specific both for the memory and for the wit. Thamus replied: O most ingenious Theuth, the parent or inventor of an art is not always the best judge of the utility

or inutility of his own inventions to the users of them. And in this instance, you who are the father of letters, from a paternal love of your own children have been led to attribute to them a quality which they cannot have; for this discovery of yours will create forgetfulness in the learners' souls, because they will not use their memories; they will trust to the external written characters and not remember of themselves. The specific which you have discovered is an aid not to memory, but to reminiscence, and you give your disciples not truth, but only the semblance of truth; they will be hearers of many things and will have learned nothing; they will appear to be omniscient and will generally know nothing; they will be tiresome company, having the show of wisdom without the reality."

Like the battle between old (autocratic) and new (democratic) systems won by the money economy, so too do we see a clash between old and new lexicology. The written word won out—despite haters like Socrates—and it's not hard to argue it set humans apart by enabling us to structure knowledge and, finally, know about knowing.

THE POWER OF THE PEN

The capacity of the written language is so great it allows the dead to speak to the living and enables perfect strangers to instantly influence one another from great distances. This "artificial memory" made history possible precisely because it transcends time and space. This should sound familiar because it's exactly what the advent of coins did for money. It is a human construct, a symbol carrying with it intrinsic value from the sender to the receiver. Because it is a system of symbols for other, unrelated things in the world around us, it is at once portable and impervious to time, and directly eliminated the last barrier preventing humans from discovering logic, mathematics, economics, medicine, and law, let alone the preservation of traditions like family history and formalized religion. The categorization of subject matter was enabled, which led to the realization of what thought is, and then, what "self" means. Logic only came into being after *logos*, Greek for "word," was adopted.

Not long after hieroglyphics were introduced, Ancient Egypt and some Mesopotamian states began using arithmetic, algebra, and geometry for commercial purposes, as well as astronomy, calendaring, and recording time. However, what the Phoenicians were to the alphabet, the Babylonians were to complex mathematics. While the former can't take credit for writing any more than the latter may lay claim to counting, both created a new system with uniform properties that could be socialized easily.

Like the money economy, writing and arithmetic were alive and kicking after becoming social phenomena. Because everyone adhered to the same rules, humans could finally share, learn from, and build on one another's work. And share they did. With conventions like letters and numbers, long-distance communications would soon follow the same development.

Like the talking drums of Cameroon, the ancient Greeks were known to use beacons of fire to rapidly pass messages long distances, as Aeschylus depicts in *Agamemnon*. After the Trojan defeat at the hands of the Greeks, news of their victory took just a few hours to travel 600 kilometers from Troy to the city of Argos:

> Leader: Say then, how long ago the city fell?

> Clytemnestra: Even in this night that now brings forth the dawn.

> Leader: Yet who so swift could speed the message here?

> Clytemnestra: From Ida's top Hephaestus, lord of fire, sent forth his sign; and on, and ever on, beacon to beacon sped the courier-flame.

Light from high places caught on as an information-dissemination technique. Stone lighthouses arose in 5th-century BCE Greece to send the unary message "Don't sail here" to passing ships. The concept played a vital role in the formation of the United States too. The binary "One if by land, two if by sea" was made famous in American elementary schools with Paul Revere's Ride after colonials hung two lanterns in the steeple of Boston's Old North Church to warn of approaching British forces. Walk through Times Square one night for evidence of its lasting power.

From smoke signals in 8th-century BCE China and ancient Rome's reflecting mirrors and carrier pigeons to the semaphore flag system in 18th-century France, narrowcasting information over long distances has saved time, energy, and indeed lives (depending on which side of the battlefield you were on). But it would not be until after the Age of Enlightenment in Europe before long-distance communications could be electrified.

While the concept of electricity had been inclined as far back as ancient Egypt, the property would remain unharnessed until Italian physicist Alessandro Volta's invention of the electric battery in 1800—eight years after Benjamin Franklin's kite and key experiment. Finally, when Volta's English contemporary Michael Faraday engineered the first generator in 1831, electromagnetism was at last ready for deploying the long-distance communication capability that would propel humanity beyond fire beacons, lighthouses, and drums forevermore.

In 1837, Sir William Cooke and Charles Wheatstone successfully installed the world's first commercial telegraph along 13 miles of the Great Western Railway from London's Paddington Station to West Drayton. That same year, Samuel Morse and his assistant Alfred Vail developed and patented their own in the United States, and with it, an original signaling code comprised of dots, dashes, and spaces between letters and words. To ensure the code they came up with demonstrated maximum efficiency and simplicity, the two visited the local paper in Morristown, New Jersey, and rummaged through the cases of movable type to assess the most- and least-used characters in the American lexicon. They found 10,000 Ts and just 200 Zs, and proceeded to optimize their Morse code accordingly. Because using a commercial telegraph cost the sender by the letter, it saved telegraphers billions of unnecessary key taps and customers the associated expense.

The first long-distance telegraph system in the US connected Washington, DC, with Baltimore using underground cables laid along the Baltimore and Ohio Railroad, a link which Morse inaugurated with the message "What hath God wrought," a phrase from the Bible's book of Numbers, in 1844. Commercial popularity soared in the States, and by 1851, Morse's system had been adopted as the European standard, leaving only Britain and its empire on the Cooke and Wheatstone method. Soon, all major cities in the eastern US were interlinked, which were in turn connected by overland cables with the West Coast in 1861, effectively killing off the Pony Express overnight. Those metal wires crisscrossing the skylines of every population center, large and small, formed what was known as an overhead "iron net work," and ultimately, "network."

Precisely because customers were charged by the letter, the emergence of the telegraph would unexpectedly change how we look at the construction of language itself. At first, people sent shorthands such as "evy" to mean "every" and "brl" to mean "barrel;" then phrases like "thank you" were truncated to "TU." This didn't make the telegraph operating companies very happy to be sure, and it wasn't long until entrepreneurs were creating code books with hundreds of shortcuts corresponding to commonly used and then even esoteric phrases. In a sort of distant precursor to the chat and texting acronyms we use today, people with the same book on either end of the line could send "5TO089R" to mean "It's a boy. Mom and baby are doing fine."

INCREMENTAL GAINS

Now, for the first time since the emergence of spoken and then written language thousands of years prior, two people could make the same association out of something completely unrelated so long as they agreed to the same terms. Furthermore, the time saved in these exchanges would enable a stratospheric rise in productivity. Trading a coin instead of growing and gathering cacao seeds had the same effect as sending a cable in moments from London to New York rather than waiting 12 days for a letter to travel the same distance, as was required in the 1860s. All that was needed was a mutually understood framework and a code to send through it.

At the same time, something brewing in Europe would lead to a dramatically more profound effect. In 1862, German inventor Philipp Reis demoed his new device for Inspector of the Royal Prussian Telegraph Corps Wilhelm von Legat. It converted sound which passed through a parchment diaphragm and transducer into electrical impulses, then transmitted them across electrical wires to another device which reconstituted them back into the sender's original acoustic signal. Reis intended to broadcast music with it. He called it *telephon*. In 1874, a Scottish-born former professor of vocal physiology and elocution at Boston University by the name of Alexander Graham Bell was attempting to develop a system which could transmit the human voice across telegraphy cables. Alongside his assistant Thomas Watson, Bell succeeded in conducting the first bidirectional transmission of intelligible speech on March 10, 1876, when he spoke into the microphone, "Mr. Watson, come here, I want to see you." He was the first to receive a patent, awarded later that year, for an "apparatus for transmitting vocal or other sounds telegraphically." The next year saw the founding of Bell Telephone Company, the world's first telephone concern, and a few after that, a subsidiary, American Telephone & Telegraph Company.

Improvements to the telephone—in particular the carbon microphone, introduced in 1877 by Thomas Edison, which was so advanced it would be used in all phones until the 1980s—as well as to the network were frequent, as adoption increased and electric power proliferated. In 1880, the

French government awarded Bell its Volta Prize along with 50,000 francs for his invention, which he spent to fund Volta Bell Laboratories in Washington, DC. After various permutations, innovation on behalf of the entire Bell System would be consolidated at Bell Laboratories, which opened its downtown Manhattan facility in 1925.

It was there that the science of information would come into its own. In 1941, a veritable intellectual goliath arrived in Claude Shannon. Shannon held a PhD in mathematics from MIT, where he designed switching circuits out of vacuum tubes that could solve Boolean algebra problems just by having them switch on or off according to "if/then" rules. His wartime work at Bell included cryptography, or the science of secure communication and hence its corollary, codebreaking. For a few months in 1943, he would meet regularly with renowned English mathematician and Enigma machine-breaker Alan Turing at teatime in the cafeteria. Turing was interested in speech encipherment and visited from DC, where he was posted to share his cryptanalytic methods with the US Navy.

Shannon's research on cryptography focused heavily on separating signal from noise, and in 1945, he released a memorandum titled *A Mathematical Theory of Cryptography*. Due to the war, it would remain classified until 1949, but its views on information theory foreshadowed the bombshell for which he is best known, *A Mathematical Theory of Communication*, widely regarded as ground zero of the information age for its analysis of the concepts of data and signal processing. In this two-part article, which appeared in the *Bell System Technical Journal*, he breaks communication down to its indivisible building blocks: binary digits, a.k.a., "bits." Just like the vacuum tubes which his system switched on and off at MIT to solve math problems, serial communication is merely a sequence of ons or offs, ones or zeros. Digital was born.

Colleague John Pierce summed up the breakthrough accurately and succinctly: "It was like a bolt from the blue." Now information theorists had much in common with physicists, in that they had their own irreducible unit. The new discipline became a bridge between mathematics and engineering. From here, language and communication had entropy, or uncertainty. Defiance of that uncertainty was signal, or information. Ioan James, who wrote Shannon's biography for the Royal Society, claimed, "So wide were its repercussions that the theory was described as one of humanity's proudest and rarest creations, a general scientific theory that could profoundly and rapidly alter humanity's view of the world." The gloves were off and the doors opened. Information had been set free.

A WEAPON, A SAVIOR

The information technologies that Shannon, Turing, and thousands of mathematicians, engineers, scientists, and theorists developed on the side of the Allies would prove the deciding blow of World War II. The Germans and Japanese had a huge head start and massive, mature war machines by the time they took the world by surprise with their respective acts of war. But it was cryptography, encoding and decoding, radar, sonar, the nuclear bomb, and even the renowned Navajo Windtalkers that dealt the historic hand. The Allies simply had more information about the Axis powers than the enemy had about them, and most importantly, the Allies could share theirs safely while the other side could not. In the end, information was the ultimate weapon that liberated millions from tyranny and ended the greatest scourge of modern civilization.

Before the war, the Josiah Macy Jr. Foundation kicked off a set of meetings in New York City called the Macy Conferences, where the greatest scientific minds from every discipline imaginable shared their research while it was still underway as opposed to after it was complete so that perspectives from a wide array of otherwise peripheral fields might accelerate problem-solving. Originally intended to stimulate medical research—the primary aim of the Macy Foundation—it morphed over time to tackle issues from across a vast spectrum, ranging from anthropology and psychology to computing and even hypnotism. Only one or two scholars from a scientific field were invited to any conference to ensure the voices on hand were broad and shallow rather than deep and narrow for maximum mental mingling.

While the subject matter during its run from 1941 to 1960 was certainly diverse, the whole affair is often lumped together today as the "Cybernetics Conferences." That's because from 1946 to 1953, ten of the symposiums were dedicated to what the godfather of the field, Norbert Wiener, described in 1948 as "the scientific study of control and communication in the animal and the machine." The oldest-known use of the word "cybernetics" was by Plato in *The Alcibiades* to signify the governance of people, but in the modern context, it came to stand for the exploration of regulatory systems. In short, of the 160 Macy Conferences held, the Cybernetics sessions were the stars of the show and ushered in a new age where the lines between mechanical engineering, biology, neuroscience, and electrical network theory muddled. It's astonishing to think this happened 65 years ago.

Unsurprisingly, we're not only built to process information, but we're made of it, as the attendees of the Cybernetic Conferences discussed. Our DNA is comprised of four nucleotide bases known as A (adenine), C (cytosine), G (guanine), and T (thymine). How those are sequenced form the foundation of our genetic code, or chromosomal makeup. Here are the first few from my DNA's nucleotide sequence: AAACGGCG. I'm not worried about what you'll do with it, as that series alone has 1,492,266 more to go, so chances are low that you'll be able to replicate me. Those letters may not be ones and zeros, but they're code all the same. As Joi, the beautiful holographic character in *Blade Runner 2049* tells her human owner: "I am just code and so are you. Mere data makes a man. A and C and T and G. The alphabet of you. All from four symbols. I am only two: 1 and 0."

EMPHASIS AND ENTROPY

In the spoken word and even African talking drum-speak, pitch and context have evolved to set intended signals apart from unintentional noise, to defeat the entropy that Claude Shannon revealed in *A Mathematical Theory of Communication*.

For example, in her *Symbols of the Eternal Doctrine: From Shamballa to Paradise*, Helen Valborg tells us about a dialect of the Bantu language spoken by the Kele people of the Democratic Republic of the Congo. Kele listeners hear homonyms and, because of the speaker's stress on one syllable, can instantly distinguish *lisaka* (marsh) from *lisaká* (promise) from *lisáká* (poison). Mispronounce *liála* (fiancée) as *liala* (garbage pit), and a Kele man can find himself in hot water. Incredibly, a skilled drummer can communicate those words clearly by hitting different areas of the drum to imitate their critical emphases—in other words, to reduce confusion, to separate signal from noise. Similarly, the Yoruba people of north-central Nigeria and their *Lya Ilu* (Mother of Drums) have an octave range that intones the subtleties between *oko* (husband), *okó* (hoe), and *óko* (canoe) when performed by an expert drummer. This happens to be the case in other ancient languages too. Far away from the African content, tonal languages like Mandarin and Cantonese employ tone to discern the tremendous disparity between *ái* (cancer) and *ài* (love), only without the drums.

Context plays a key role here too. If a speaker or drummer doesn't perfectly nail the critical point of emphasis, the words preceding and following the one in question help to sort signal from noise. So if a Kele man is thought to have said—or drummed—"I can't wait to marry you, garbage pit," the listener has other associated data to guide her to the intended information. It's also important to know the receiver's own personal context, which has the power to distort the original message in ways wholly unanticipated by the sender.

When I learned the above a few years ago, I looked for an opportunity to perform an experiment on context in terms of a listener's perspective. In the Amazon London office, we usually had streaming radio playing in the ADX area. One afternoon, I got my chance, as the first track from The Prodigy's 1996 LP *The Fat of the Land* blared from the speaker with the opening phrase "Change my pitch up." Across my desk sat a Brit and an American, whom I asked what that line meant to them. The British guy said, "I dunno. He's a singer, so I just assumed he was talking about changing the pitch of his voice up." The American responded, "I thought it was a reference to a change-up pitch in baseball." Same line, distinct mental contexts, completely different meanings. A simple example, but it proved to me that one must know his listener—his *customer*—to increase the odds that the intended message sent is the one received.

EVERY WORD MATTERS

As I've implored the writers on my teams over the years, every word matters. Whether or not you're paid to write or speak copy, words are deployed by the human mind to serve clarity and retention first. Redundancy, considered an inefficiency in most systems, can help provide that clarity if used strategically. We've all heard the presentation rule, "Tell them what you are going to tell them, tell them, then tell them what you told them." Know who made that up? The grand master of rhetoric, Aristotle. In the right places, redundancy is actually more efficient, because it saves the customer of your information-exchange both time and energy. Clear communication is, at its core, customer-obsessed.

A good example is the International Radiotelephony Spelling Alphabet, a.k.a., the International Civil Aviation Organization (ICAO) phonetic alphabet or NATO phonetic alphabet. With the rapid increase in international air travel over the last century, the ICAO sought a simple way to ensure clear air-to-ground radio communication that would work globally. After extensive research by the US military and Harvard's Psycho-Acoustic Laboratory, they assigned the clearest, least ambiguous word to each letter of the alphabet so soldiers could understand when using "military interphones in the intense noise encountered in modern warfare." The result: "AL-FAH" for "A," "BRAH-VOH" for "B," and so on. Whether you're yelling coordinates in battle, landing a plane carrying 400 passengers, or sending an email to colleagues, remember that taking an extra moment to maximize clarity saves everyone time and can go a long way to building customer loyalty.

Now, as I mentioned at the top of this chapter, I firmly believe information is the most powerful currency. Its flexibility is vast, from enlightenment to ransom and, as such, it can be weaponized. On April 23, 2013, a 12-word tweet went out on the Associated Press's Twitter account that read, "Breaking: Two Explosions in the White House and Barack Obama is injured." For the next six minutes, the world and the US stock market in particular went haywire. When all was said and done, the market dropped and then quickly recovered $136.5 billion in capitalization. Of course, it was a hack, and no explosions ever occurred in Obama's White House, but the seismic reaction was no less real. Each word tweeted by the Syrian Electronic Army, which claimed responsibility, was temporarily worth $11.375 billion. Costlier words were never typed.

The event also shed light on programmatic trading programs that use algorithms to monitor digital news sources and initiate trades according to predetermined rules. Now if you think $11 billion's a lot, allow me to refer you to May 6, 2010, when at 2:42 p.m., all major stock indices took a nosedive amounting to a trillion dollars. The Flash Crash, as it came to be known, lasted 36 minutes, long enough to become the second-largest intraday point swing in Dow Jones Industrial Average history: 1,010.14 points. The ensuing SEC/CFTC report blamed high-frequency trading (HFT) programs: "Still lacking sufficient demand from fundamental buyers or cross-market arbitrageurs, HFTs began to quickly buy and then resell contracts to each other—generating a 'hot-potato' volume effect as the same positions were rapidly passed back and forth. Between 2:45:13 and 2:45:27, HFTs traded over 27,000 contracts, which accounted for about 49 percent of the total trading volume, while buying only about 200 additional contracts net." According to the *New York Times*, this "caused shares of some prominent companies like Procter &

Gamble and Accenture to trade down as low as a penny or as high as $100,000."

Your mobile phone agreement is called a data plan for a reason. Gone forever are the communication systems which charged by the minute, as it was for decades. The exchange of data is where the money's at. In fact, I happily pay 1/2.91666667-to-the-seventh-power of 1 cent for every 1 or 0 that I consume monthly. (I really should get an unlimited plan.)

OF ONES AND ZEROS, BULLDOZERS AND BULLETS

Data are powerful and all-pervasive such that they're transforming the surface of the earth, especially when the time and money currencies get involved. In 2007, a guy named Dan Spivey had an idea—exploit the microdiscrepancies (the spread) between the cost of futures contracts in Chicago and their underlying equities in New York City using an ultra-low-latency (i.e., close to the speed of light) fiber line between the two trading centers. The concept was sound, but Spivey was not successful in gaining access to the lowest-latency pipe available at the time. So he decided to build his own and looked for investors to pay for it.

Enter former Netscape CEO James Barksdale, with whom Spivey cofounded Spread Networks. By March 2009, the company had 125 construction crews digging ditches alongside state roads, boring tunnels under rivers, and sawing through the Allegheny Mountains to make way for the one-inch line, laid as straight as possible on its 825-mile passage. When the cable, which *Forbes* estimated cost around $300 million to build, was complete, a signal could make the circuit from Chicago to New York and back again in 13.33 milliseconds, roughly 3 milliseconds faster than the next-lowest-latency line. Those three-thousandths of a second are an eternity in the HTF world and worth infinite sums. The connection is known as "dark fiber," meaning it is leased, so you have to pay to play. And pay they do. As Jon Najarian, cofounder of market intelligence site OptionMonster, put it, "Anybody pinging both markets has to be on this line, or they're dead." Information, meet time and money.

What else can ones and zeroes do today that they couldn't do before? Well for starters, they can kill you. In 2013, a young Texan named Cody Wilson fired the first fully 3D-printed gun. After it didn't explode on the remote testing stand, he hightailed it back to Austin to upload the blueprints to his website for anyone to download. In less than a week, however, the authorities came calling, claiming he'd run afoul of International Trade in Arms Regulations for exporting firearms without a license. Next, in an act of genuine libertarian defiance, Wilson took the State Department to court, citing that computer code is a form of speech and the government was violating *his* inalienable rights to both bear arms and share information. In 2015, he won a settlement in a landmark ruling that would forever bind the First and Second Amendments.

When most of us hear data mentioned in the news, we tend to think of personally identifiable information (PII) because of high-profile breaches like the one perpetrated upon Yahoo, which impacted 3 billion user accounts. While a hacker stealing your address and credit card number can't physically harm you like a 3D-printed gun, it's painful nonetheless. A fraudulent purchase made in your name is a nuisance that forces you to call the issuer, refute the purchase, and cancel your card, but it's rarely so damaging to your credit rating or reputation that it warrants avoiding credit cards altogether. Then there's the big guns of PII—your social security number (here in the US), bank account info, email and social login credentials, health records, and address history, which enable anyone in their possession to assume your identity, do whatever they want as "you," and pretty much ruin your entire life. These PII data are stored on any number of corporate and governmental servers of varying levels of security, all around the world, and managed by people you don't know. Hackers like those in Russia's elite Unit 26165, or the ones lurking on the dark web as you read this, salivate over these treasure troves which stand to both enrich themselves and threaten huge companies, governments, and even the economy itself.

The day of reckoning was an eventuality, and it came on

May 25, 2018. Information of such grave importance to millions of citizens, kept in environments lacking universal standards and provisions of control for the subjects of the data, prompted the EU Commission to issue the General Data Protection Regulation (GDPR). Its first line: "The protection of natural persons in relation to the processing of personal data is a fundamental right." The basic PII covered are name, photo, email address, social media posts, personal medical information, IP addresses, and bank details. What's more, Article 9 of GDPR outlines those data considered particularly sensitive and requiring extra security, like race or ethnicity, religious or spiritual beliefs, political or philosophical leanings, trade union alliances, biological/genetic data, medical data, and sexuality/gender identity, as misuse of these data points could render the subject vulnerable to bias, attack, or exploitation.

The FAANG companies (Facebook, Apple, Amazon, Netflix, and Google) and their contemporaries may be headquartered in the US, but if they want to operate anywhere in the EU, they must comply with the regulations or face hefty fines. Hopefully the measures they take in the EU are contagious and extend to their policies worldwide. In some ways, it feels like a zero-sum game, in that everyone from policymakers and corporate CEOs to Peter and Paula Public is at risk. We're all in this together.

Atossa Araxia Abrahamian, the author of a book about

emerging types of citizenship, *The Cosmopolites*, summed it up well in an opinion piece in the *New York Times* a few days after GDPR went live: "In broader terms, the regulation is an attempt to make sense of newly complex and decentralized relationships among individuals, their data, the state and the private sector that have emerged under globalization…. We should all start thinking of ourselves not just as clients of a company, residents of a state or citizens of a country, but also as data subjects of the world. Data is currency; creating and holding it is power. This power has gone to Google, Facebook, Amazon, and the other neo-feudal masters that use it to their advantage, not ours."

Tighter reins around how organizations capture, store, use, share, and dispose of data will have consequences for every company, especially social networks, which traffic in user-generated content. That's the GDPR Article 9 stuff, like political beliefs and sexual orientation. Anything that constrains Facebook's data—er, money—supply directly affects the long-term viability of its business model. Social networks are in a more tenuous position than most because they're simultaneously data controllers (they handle personal data) and data processors (they process personal data for other data controllers). To Facebook CEO Mark Zuckerberg, your information is way more valuable than your money. Advertisers pay billions to use it to target you with their ads. You need only provide your name and email address and then consent to the privacy policy. With that seemingly innocuous bit of info, you've purchased access to Facebook, billions of possible connections, and a universe of content. Facebook doesn't want your money. It needs your email address, password, and cat videos.

Despite its Wall Street woes in the fallout of the Cambridge Analytica scandal, Facebook's numbers still outrun the rest of the economy by a sizable distance. In its Q3 2018 earnings call, it reported profits of $5.78 billion and an operating margin of 42 percent—twice that of most IT firms in the S&P 500 and four times the margin of the entire index. Facebook might argue these staggering profits are the result of the vision of its leadership and the brilliance of its engineers, but that reasoning conveniently omits a critical truth: Facebook draws in much more money than it spends because it doesn't have to pay for its most essential asset. *The Economist* wrote in 2017 that data has replaced oil as the world's most valuable resource. It is the fuel for every digital service, which is practically any entity of import today. Facebook and other digital empires get it from us free of charge. That's another slam-dunk reason why information is a currency.

Unfortunately, I'm not convinced everyone is aware of the risks of not taking PII security ultra-seriously. It might just be a generational thing. Anyone born before 1980 remembers life before the internet; those who came after, for the most part, do not. Education consultant Marc Prensky popularized the terms "Digital Immigrant" and "Digital Native" to define the generational divide in a 2001 article. I prefer calling the younger group "screenagers" because everything they know and trust comes from a device with a backlit display. Emphasis on "know" and "trust." If a younger person has never suffered a data security attack or compromise of personal information, they are far more likely to just assume "It'll never happen to me"—as youth have been wont to do since the dawn of time—and run the risk of negatively altering the long life they have ahead of them.

Similarly, those on the older end of the spectrum may suffer from spending most of their lives as the Receiver in Marshall McLuhan's one-way sender-receiver model. In his 1964 book *Understanding Media: The Extensions of Man* (where he introduced the famous aphorism "The medium is the message"), McLuhan claims prophetically, "We live mythically and integrally...but continue to think in the old, fragmented space and time patterns of the pre-electric age." That statement is dead-on today if you replace "electric" with "internet" when considering the media-consumption habits of the older generation, whose tendency may be to forget that today's is a two-way street. Not everything they see online is trustworthy, as it (mostly) was in the days of three national TV networks. Moreover, they may not be aware of the sheer volume of data about themselves they're willfully divulging, let alone what the technologically advanced are using it for. That's a consideration that didn't exist before the internet took over our lives.

WHAT'S IT ALL MEAN TO YOU?

Thankfully, not everyone on the receiving end of our data wants to take advantage of us. Take, for instance, the Internet of Things (IoT) revolution. With our personal data, preferences, purchases, considerations, medical histories, and more, connected machines are in the process of gaining the ability to hypertailor our immediate environments. Today, we speak to voice assistants like Amazon Alexa (named for the world's first great library, Alexandria), but soon, we will be our own data objects in an ambient environment that will detect everything from our mood and body temperature to the medications we take, and then customize the physical setting automatically without our having to say a word or touch an interface. If Elon Musk's new company Neuralink has its way, we'll have brain implants that activate sensors in the surfaces of walls, furniture, counters, our cars, and more to save time by having things prepared before we even arrive at our destination. The concept of "everyware," or ubiquitous computing, is coming with the help of improved battery power, infrared, radio-frequency identification, and wireless protocols like Bluetooth, ZigBee, and Thread that will be embedded in everything, even trees and cyborg "insects" currently in development. Always-on health monitoring will help us move from reactive, centralized health care at a hospital after a physical issue arises to preventive wellness. If developed with selflessness and genuine empathy, the future can be promising, particularly for the blind, deaf, and elderly, who will live much richer lives because of it.

As I mentioned in chapter 2, at Amazon, data is all-pervasive. There, it is used to innovate and proactively serve the customer. And sure, it's also deployed to target ads but, with the richness of its purchase and browsing behavior, does so with a remarkable degree of relevance to each customer's demonstrated behavior. This commitment extends to the Amazon employee, whose responsibility it is to supply the data that leaders and operations can use to streamline the business for maximum efficiency and keep costs as low as possible. Everyone is also held to a high standard of self- and team-performance using these data. Remember, at Amazon, if it can't be proven with data, it never happened.

With so much information around, winning attention is getting expensive. In the words of Frank Zappa, "Information is not knowledge, and knowledge is not wisdom." Just because you put something out there doesn't mean it reached its destination, was understood, or valued. That puts the onus on us to offer information and experiences with real, customer-first meaning and significance. When you offer tangible meaning (signal) amid the commotion (noise), people will be drawn to you without thinking about it. Their attraction will be organic, because they're likely not getting anything important from most other sources. That means their appreciation stands a good chance of being authentic too.

Alas, most brands have quite a distance to go in that department. Don't just take my word for it. Ask Parisian philosopher and cybernetics historian Jean-Pierre Dupuy. "The more we 'communicate' the way we do, the more we create a hellish world," he wrote. "A paradox is at work here: ours is a world about which we pretend to have more and more information but which seems to us increasingly devoid of meaning."

CHAPTER 8

———

Information and the Customer

"People believe they last forever and words are temporary, when it's the opposite that's true."

—UNCLE MILT

The candle flickered in the corner of the dark tent where the boy's father lay on his deathbed. From outside, the son pulled apart the flaps of goat-hair fabric and slowly entered the shelter.

"My father," the boy whispered.

"Here I am. Who are you, my son?" asked the man, his eyes still shut.

"I am Esau, your firstborn," the boy responded. "I have done as you told me; now sit up and eat of my game, that your soul may bless me."

"Please come near, that I may feel you, my son," the man beckoned, "to know whether you are really my son Esau or not."

So Jacob went near to Isaac, his father, who felt him and said, "The voice is Jacob's voice, but the hands are the hands of Esau. Are you really my son Esau?"

Jacob answered, "I am."

And there, in chapter 27 of the book of Genesis, we have the first recorded act of identity theft. Jacob took advantage of his father Isaac's fading eyesight to secure his slightly older twin's birthright, which awarded the firstborn son the family inheritance. As Isaac neared his final hours, he asked Esau to go hunt for a special meal, after which he would bless him. When Rebekah, Isaac's wife and the boys' mother, overheard this, she helped her favored son disguise himself as Esau and bring the dying father the meal while his brother was still out in the wilderness.

Jacob isn't alone in history in assuming someone else's identity for personal gain. In the Wild West and, later, the bootleg mobster era of the early 1920s, outlaws killed people and assumed their identities to remain a step ahead of the authorities. Professional identity thieves have captured our imagination in pop culture too, as in the films *The Talented Mr. Ripley* and *Catch Me If You Can*, because it's just so brazen. The lead character in the greatest TV series ever (author's opinion), *Mad Men*, Donald Draper was actually a man named Dick Whitman who assumed his lieutenant's identity by switching dog tags with his superior's charred remains after an ambush in the Korean War.

All of those events, fictional or non-, shared one key characteristic: they preceded the computer age. If you had the chutzpah and cunning, it was relatively easy to pretend to be someone you're not because verification systems relied on paper and ink (or poor eyesight), which could be easily circumvented. You'd be within your rights to believe, then, that the computer would have made it much harder to succeed as an ID thief. In many ways, like with retina and fingerprint scanning, you're correct. But in the majority of other areas, it has been simplified. By 2015, identity theft was the most-filed complaint submitted to the US Federal Trade Commission for the trailing 15 years.

That's because our identities—or hallways to them—are now needed to gain entry onto the web, where all of our private business is carried out. An individual or small group of uber-expert hackers will always be more nimble than, say, Citibank because they're free to try and try again. The criminals only have to be right once, whereas Citi and its thousands of human (i.e., error-prone) employees have to be right 100 percent of the time. Plus, the hackers' only expense is time, a cheap computer, the cost of an internet connection, junk food, and *Star Wars* T-shirts. (I suppose there's also that pesky chance of getting caught, but it's exceedingly rare because digitally covering his tracks is a hacker's first order of business.)

Thus, we pay to use Twitter with our data—a username and password. It may not sound like a lot, but possessing just one correct set of those credentials is a boon to a hacker because most people use the same password, or a slight variant of it, on every site they join. That's right, the majority of web users have the same username/password combo for their banks, credit cards, food delivery services, social networks, and shopping sites. Plus, "123456" is still the number one password, followed by "123456789" and "qwerty," so hackers start with a dictionary of hundreds of the most-used passwords and hit pay dirt a lot more often than you'd imagine. Get one right, and a "black hat" likely has the garage-door opener to your entire life.

Once a customer goes online, there are two primary types of information she generates: explicit and implicit. Explicit data are generated by a user intentionally, like a social post, taking a survey, or entering a sweepstakes. The longest-standing kinds of implicit online data, which are mined from explicit data, are browsing and purchase behavior.

That person is merely going about her business like shopping or reading the news and, in doing so, is being monitored by a server and database somewhere about how long she remained on a particular page (called "dwell time"), what she searched for, what she put in her shopping cart, what she removed from that cart, and all other products she considered before checking out.

But it doesn't stop there. The explicit data in a social post offers another layer of implicit data that can be garnered by a skillful operator. Let's make up a post from a woman named Gloria: "Checking out of office early today to hit Billy's Burger Shack with my BFF @LisaBee1213! #sorrynotsorry" offers a ream of secondary data: (1) Gloria has a day job, probably at a white-collar company with an office, (2) she's achieved a professional status sufficient to allow her to leave early to spend time with a friend and openly boast about it, (3) she has a typical office departure time, (4) she went to work today, (5) the women are best friends, (6) Gloria has a high affinity for the restaurant, (7) they are almost certainly not vegetarians, and (8) their office is probably not far from Billy's Burger Shack.

As such, we are simultaneously data factories and data mines. We manufacture incredible amounts of information by doing the least remarkable things on our computers and connected devices, and companies mine it for enormous financial gain. We are paying with and giving away significant sums of one currency, information, and big tech takes it and converts it into another, money. All of that posting you do on Facebook, searching on Google, watching on Netflix, and shopping on Amazon sets up millions of demographic and psychographic associations that marketers pay dearly to access to ensure the relevance of their ads. Hitting the right customer with the right message at the right time saves advertisers money by reducing wasted spend (i.e., serving an ad to the wrong person), and drives revenue after a sale. Therefore, the company with the largest, deepest data set and the most products that advertisers can pay to use wins.

Some companies are turning the tide from this one-way transaction model, where you're an ATM, into a more equitable two-way exchange for explicit data. Steemit is a social network that pays you in their cryptocurrency, Steem, when you post to your blog in their space. The more reads, upvotes, and shares your posts earn, the more Steem you're awarded. Similarly, Storyful was founded in Dublin, Ireland, by journalists who saw an opportunity to break news faster by finding user-generated video content as it happens, verifying and licensing it from the person who posted it, and then paying her for it. Because we all have camera phones on our persons at all times, eyewitnesses to natural disasters, crimes, and other newsworthy items stand to profit by being on-hand well before a news crew can show up and capture the aftermath. It was so smart and effective that Rupert Murdoch's News Corp. bought the company in 2013 for $25 million, and it now sells content to news outlets, advertisers, and any other company that wants to take advantage of authentic, in-the-moment video.

Naturally, different big tech entities specialize in different areas of customer data. From experience, I see a rather substantial difference between Google's and Amazon's primary data offerings. Here's an example using myself and my twin brother. Anthony and I share a lifetime of near-identical experiences, personal histories, education, family members, friends, and interests. However, to a search engine, Anth and I are much more similar data objects than what an e-commerce environment sees in our implicit and explicit data. I should start by telling you that he's a husband and father of two little ones living in suburban Columbus, Ohio, and I'm a single guy living in Manhattan. Google knows us both as people who searched "Who was defensive MVP in the controversial 1973 Ohio State-Michigan game?" To Amazon, we are similar in some areas, like browsing and buying the latest tech gadgets, but only he purchases child car seats and toddler golf club sets. Now, Google certainly has an incredible data set on each of us so my example is simpleminded, and I admit I'm not giving them their full credit due, but even so, there is a legitimate distinction about us as data objects revealed by what we search versus what we buy. Purchase data more clearly tell the world—and ad servers and algorithms—who we really are (or want to be). That chasm appears to be widening. In September 2018, a report from

Adeptmind found that 46.7 percent of US internet users start their product searches at Amazon to Google's 34.6 percent. For purchasing, Amazon isn't just where we buy, it's where we learn, and that's a powerful proposition. (Oh, and the defensive MVP was Arnie Jones.)

WHERE RATINGS AND REVIEWS RULE

One of the main contributors to Amazon's popularity is its customer reviews. In the field of psychology, there's a principal known as social proof, a.k.a., informational social influence, which asserts that when humans face ambiguity, they assume the actions of the others around them. Social proof is what happens in crowds when someone standing by himself collapses to the ground in full view of everybody, yet no one runs to help him. If no individual rushes to aid the victim—who's there alone without anyone to instantly call for help—the witnesses carry on with whatever they were doing because no one else acted. It is so mysteriously potent that people have died in the midst of hundreds of other crowd members because of the effect social proof has on us. Unsurprisingly, social proof works in less critical scenarios, like online shopping. If I'm ambiguous about which product to buy, I look to what others are buying. Those star ratings—the selfsame reviews that angered the publisher in chapter 2—make a huge difference precisely because of social proof. Amazon tells its advertisers to include customer reviews of 3.5 stars or better in their advertisements to raise the campaign's click-through and conversions rates. Both Amazon and the LGs, Fitbits, and Gatorades of the world benefit greatly from these explicit data which customers post in reviews (if the product's good, that is).

Aside from customer reviews and word-of-mouth, the other ways customers tend to learn about your brand are from social media and news coverage, which typically magnify mistakes and downplay successes. You're definitely playing to a tough crowd, and it's only getting more difficult as new options and voices come online. Finally, the most fundamental of all: one's own sensory information gathered during shopping, demonstrating, and using the product or service itself. This is the major barrier for the online grocery industry, which eMarketer estimated in an October 2018 report represents just 2.8 percent of all e-commerce purchases worldwide and 1.6 percent in the US. Pharmaceuticals aside, people prefer to investigate visually, tactically, audibly, and olfactorily what they're about to put inside their bodies. Alas, squeezing avocados and tapping honeydews is tough to do from your desktop.

In closing, we as customers own our minds and bodies, so shouldn't that apply to the information they generate? It appears the Europeans think so. Over the long term, I believe strongly we'll begin to see brands going over and above to demonstrate respect for not just protecting their customers' data—taking a half-hearted approach will destroy any company over time, no matter how successful—but offering transparency and even sharing the wealth it produces, à la Steemit. Taking a little off the bottom line to create a responsible data partnership with customers will transform good brands into great and ensure longevity for those committed to it. We've all read what happens when they don't.

CHAPTER 9

Information and the Brand

"New ideas are merely words on a blind date."

—UNCLE MILT

The young man walked briskly down the wide, arched hallway, doing his physical best not to run, which is not permitted inside the Central Administrative Okrug—certainly not for a Center 18 contractor anyway. The corridor, with its Baroque vaulted ceilings, pale green walls accented with alabaster and gold leaf, and 20-foot-wide lighting rotundas overhead, had more in common with a train station than an office building. A run-of-the-mill work environment this was not. Opened in 1898 to house the insurance company Rossiya, it would later come to be associated with something considerably more sinister. By 2013, the building's former KGB tenants were gone, but their successors, the Federal Security Service of the Russian Federation (FSB), enjoyed the imposing facility as their headquarters in Lubyanka Square, about 1,000 yards from Red Square.

The 26-year-old with unmanaged hair and a bulbous nose rounded a corner, made a beeline to a door, and knocked gently. "входить," he heard from inside. "Come in." He turned the knob, slipped inside, and closed it quietly behind him. In muted, hurried Russian, he let fly a torrent of news that could be summed up with just six English words, "Forb, I think we've done it."

Dmitry Dokuchaev went by the same alias, Forb, throughout his black-hat career. After he was nabbed for credit card fraud by the FSB, the Russian authorities gave him one chance to make his woes disappear: work for their Center for Information Security, a.k.a., Center 18, or face hard time in Lefortovo Prison across town. As an officer at Center 18, Forb had contracted Alexsey Belan, the man in his office, and a 22-year-old Kazakhstan-born Canadian citizen named Karim Baratov to penetrate the computer systems of major American companies on behalf of the Russian government. That day, they did it.

PRIVACY POLICIES: THE GOOD, THE BAD, THE BREACHED

It would be four years until Yahoo and American officials would uncover the full extent of the hack—three billion accounts in total, the largest in history. By that point, all three of the agents and a fellow officer, Igor Sushchin, were locked up. Dokuchaev, Sushchin, and Belan sit accused of double-crossing Russia by carrying out missions with the CIA, while Baratov was sentenced to five years in a US prison with a $250,000 fine awaiting his release.

Google got hit too but immediately doubled-down with hundreds of millions of dollars in investments in data security infrastructure and engineers dedicated to the task, under the internal tagline, "Never Again." In September 2016, the *New York Times* reported that Yahoo was not as quick to act. According to six then-current and former employees, CEO Marissa Mayer prioritized design improvements in areas like Yahoo Mail and new product development over security enhancements. The argument of "too expensive" undermined the efforts of the Paranoids, the security division's internal moniker, to secure funding for their objectives. The brand paid the penultimate price and, in 2017, was purchased by Verizon for $4.48 billion. Today it is a shadow of its former self.

In the earlier section on the money currency, I asked, "What are you doing with your customer's money?" Even though it supports your company's bottom line, it should never be considered as "yours." It's theirs, and it's on loan. The same goes for their data. How are you using—no, *earning and spending* your customer's information? At Amazon, every employee is

drilled with a near-religious fervor on the ultimate importance of data protection for exactly the Yahoo reason cited.
Protecting your customer's info is protecting your business.

A note on privacy policies, which most people don't bother
to read when registering to use an app or website. Have
you read your brand's? I mean, *really* read it, top to bottom,
slowly, like you mean it? That's what I thought. The next
time you have a spare hour (or for many sites, even longer),
get out a magnifying glass and pore over it, as if you were
your customer. Do you understand it all or at least most of it?
That's also what I thought. Do your brand a favor and create a
second, humanistically written privacy policy. Of course, the
technical one that Legal wrote will have to remain up, but
if you care about your customer, give her the scoop in con-
versational English and have the other one just a click away.
The irony is that privacy policies are purposely written so that
laypeople can't understand them, which I find despicable.
You might be thinking, "But that's Legal's jurisdiction," to
which I say, "Shame on you, Legal. You're being self-obsessed,
not customer-obsessed."

On April 10, 2018, a visibly tense Mark Zuckerberg sat before
the Senate Judiciary and Commerce committees in Washington, DC, to take questions related to what he and his company
knew about the Cambridge Analytica reports in relation to
President Trump's election campaign. One of my favorite
parts of the whole circus—aside from the spectacle of 60- and

70-year-olds with no technical experience discussing subject matter they barely understand—was this exchange between the Facebook CEO and Republican Senator from Wisconsin Ron Johnson:

Johnson: Thank you, Mr. Zuckerberg, for testifying here today. Do you have any idea how many of your users actually read the terms of service, the privacy policy, the statement of rights and responsibilities? I mean, actually read it?

Zuckerberg: Senator, I do not.

Johnson: Would you imagine it's a very small percentage?

Zuckerberg: Senator, who read the whole thing? I would imagine that probably most people do not read the whole thing. But everyone has the opportunity to and consents to it.

Johnson: Well, I agree. But that's kind of true of every application where, you know, you want to get to it and you have to agree to it, and people just press that "agree"—the vast majority, correct?

Zuckerberg: Senator, it's really hard for me to make a full assessment, but...

Johnson: Common sense would tell you that would be probably the case.

I burst out laughing at the senator's interruption because the truth behind the privacy policy has never been about protecting the user but rather the company, and this guy just told it like it is in front of the whole world. News flash for Mr. Zuckerberg: IT'S YOUR COMPANY. You can make that change with a snap of your fingers. Make it so people will *want* to read it. Next time you (the reader, not Zuckerberg) fly United Airlines (Zuck flies private), watch their flight safety video before takeoff for living proof that serious can be fun. They're cute and genuinely funny, and I actually find myself hoping a new one's been made since my last flight. Turning something I dread into what I enjoy? That's customer-obsessed and fantastic branding.

Now then, this chapter is about much more than how brands do or don't safeguard their customers' information. When we consider the change in how customers receive information about brands and their products over the past decade, the advantage is decidedly *not* on the side of the brand, which enjoyed McLuhan's strict sender-receiver model until the digital upheaval. Sure, there are time-honored corporate communications including marketing, advertising, websites, press releases, and investor relations, but those tend to be one-sided by nature. Rarely are those communications customer-first, so they're usually ignored as self-serving until verified by someone we know and trust—or, as in the case of Amazon's customer reviews, total strangers with little to gain by lying. At odds with the half-truths spun by so many advertisers is real-life customer experience. How many times have you watched TV with someone who called out a commercial as "total BS"? No amount of advertising spend is going to change that, at least for that one person's experience. The problem is that now it's affected two audience members, because I'll take my sister's word over a 30-second litany of some brand's self-absorption any day.

TWO SIDES OF TRANSPARENCY

Naturally, every business has information about itself it must keep confidential, by law or otherwise, so where do we as brand owners draw the line between overdivulging and brand transparency? Paid marketing is designed to sell a brand's products as well as, sometimes, the brand itself. Other corporate communications are intended to take a straighter line with information aimed at regulators, corporate partners, the press, and the omnipresent shareholder. Who makes the decision about which information to share (spend) and with whom? In my experience, it's usually the legal department, which is there, by definition, to protect the company, so the information about your brand will almost certainly not be customer-centric.

In the end, it comes down to the ideals the company behind the brand has, if they have any formalized values at all, and how well they're instilled and demonstrated by employees and leadership. Just like people, companies with a lot to hide are forced to hand the reins to legal when making their information-spending decisions, practically guaranteeing low brand equity with customers. What comes around goes around.

On the other side of that coin is Patagonia, the sustainable outdoor apparel brand out of Ventura, California, which in November 2018 announced it would donate the $10 million payout it received from the GOP's corporate tax break to environmental nonprofits. By clinging steadfastly to its eco-sensitive ideals in everything it does, it has earned immense loyalty, which endows the brand with license to spend much more information about itself than most companies, in turn driving even higher loyalty. The centerpiece of its environmental and social responsibility efforts is the Footprint Chronicles at Patagonia.com, which openly showcases details on every product's origin and the journey through the supply chain from the cotton field or recycling facility to the store rack or warehouse. Click on a ski jacket or pair of board shorts and right there, on the product detail page, sits the "View the Footprint Chronicles" link. Clicking on it sends the customer to slideshows, videos, and interviews covering everything from the clothing designer's rationale for selecting the polyester made from recycled plastic bottles to the carbon footprint of the freight ship from China.

According to Patagonia's VP of environmental initiatives Rick Ridgeway, the Footprint Chronicles is the brand's opportunity to "discuss what is good about the product and what sucks." As he told *Fast Company* in 2011, "By being transparent with you, we can invite you into the conversation. On the Footprint Chronicles, there is a place to let us know what you think, or if you have any better ideas on how to make our products." Talk about humility. Nice guys (and brands) can finish first.

Contrast that with lux brands like Dior and Longchamp, which earned a 0 out of a possible 100 percent score on the 2018 Fashion Transparency Index, a joint project between UK nonprofit Fashion Revolution and research cooperative Ethical Consumer, which ranks "150 of the biggest global fashion brands and retailers...according to how much they disclose about their social and environmental policies, practices, and impact." (To be perfectly candid, I was surprised to see Amazon scored a dismal 10 in the same survey.)

The industry panel assigns up to 250 points along five categories: policy and commitments; governance; traceability; know, show, and fix; and spotlight issues. Founder and global operations director of Fashion Revolution Carry Somers was motivated to do something after the April 23, 2013, collapse of a garment factory in Dhaka, Bangladesh, killed 1,134 employees and injured thousands more. The disaster prompted brands around the world to investigate their hundreds and even thousands of manufacturing and supply chain relationships to see if their garments were made there. For most of them, it took weeks to find out. You know globalization in the fashion world is positively byzantine when the brands themselves don't even know where their stuff is being made.

Further on in the index, under the heading "People want to know #whomademyclothes," the authors state, "Consumers don't want to buy clothes made by people working in danger, exploited, paid poverty-level wages, in polluted environments, but there is simply not enough information available about the clothes we wear." It also quotes a 2016 stat from Havas that we should all take to heart and apply to every brand, not just fashion: "In a survey of over 10,000 consumers from around the world, 78 percent said it is somewhat or very important for a company to be transparent." We should begin to consider ways to ease our organizations out of the darkness before our blemishes are exposed in broad daylight. In other words, it's way better to ask a customer for permission than forgiveness. It's the least we can do for the very people supplying us with all of *their* information.

At Amazon, customers generate mind-blowing amounts of data every day, not just on special events like Prime Day 2018, when the company announced that Prime members in 17 countries purchased more than 100 million products—including 300,000 Instant Pots and 150,000 LifeStraws—making it the biggest shopping event in its history. I used to joke that capturing and analyzing all this browsing and buying behavior makes NASA look like Cracker Barrel by comparison. Every day, the system gets smarter about you to accomplish its primary goal of better servicing the customer with technologies like predictive modeling, strategic inventory, and logistics. It also results in more relevant ad-serving so that I don't get the banner for child car seats that my brother gets, wasting that advertiser's money and annoying me with its irrelevance.

Like many tech companies, Amazon has five classifications for its data that are repeated non-stop from an employee's first day: public, confidential, highly confidential, restricted, and critical. I don't think I ever saw anything more sensitive than confidential during my tenure because it's on a strictly need-to-know basis, and I was an advertising creative about a thousand light-years away from a need to know. When I first started there, friends and family used to ask me if I could pull up their orders on some internal database and spy on their activities, to which I'd scoff, "You don't know Amazon."

THE SCOOP ON SENTIMENT AND FEEDBACK

Another way companies receive information from customers is the brand sentiment survey, where researchers poll thousands of respondents in one or more geographies on the brands they believe live up to their promises, demonstrate a commitment to customer service, exhibit corporate responsibility, and other data points. (Amazon routinely does well on these, topping many through the years.) The surreptitious cousin of brand sentiment research is social sentiment analysis, where similar investigators scrape social networks and analyze every mention of the brand they can find and assign a positive, negative, or neutral rating to them. These you should take with a grain of salt unless the score is overwhelming in either direction.

In a June 2017 *Journal of Advertising Research* report on a study by Engagement Labs, researchers showed that online sentiment around the Dick's Sporting Goods move to cease selling assault rifles and mandate gun buyers be 21 was met negatively in the social sphere but positively offline. If you engage in social language-mining for your brand, you have to be prepared to be both continuously vigilant and patient, as *Forbes* proved with Nike and its campaign featuring Colin Kaepernick. Hours after it launched, the mood online was loud and angry, but in the matter of just two days, it turned and remained positive. If Nike had limited its monitoring to the initial reaction, they'd have deprived themselves of a powerful insight they can use on future campaigns.

At Amazon, the phrase "feedback is a gift" is jokingly dropped from time to time, ostensibly after someone somewhere in the company said it seriously. While we sarcastically echoed the line to each other, feedback is actually an all-consuming proposition there. The company takes every opportunity it can find across its universe to plead for and enable instant feedback from customers and business partners alike. Moments after I sign for a Prime Now delivery, I receive a confirmation on the phone app with a feedback button. Accompanying every display ad on desktop and mobile is an Ad Feedback link which allows me to comment on the relevance of the unit and how appropriate it is, with a form for open-ended comments. And believe me when I say it is read and taken seriously. Additionally, with every end-of-campaign report sent to their clients, Amazon Advertising account executives include a link to enter a Net Promoter Score (NPS). The NPS is the industry standard in customer sentiment via the likelihood of someone recommending your company. The NPS score is a key feature of internal reporting at Amazon, and improving it is the target of programs throughout the enterprise.

ALL ABOUT IP (IN ACTION)

Finally, intellectual property (IP) is a critically important form of information for brands. What is a new idea but someone making an original association between two seemingly unrelated pieces of information? Combining data, the LPs (indexing heavily on Think Big and Invent and Simplify), programs, and goals within a customer-obsessed culture is the story of Amazon's success. And all of it is predicated on the internal exchange of information.

I was fortunate to have started a program with an ambitious, highly technical objective in a field I was absolutely unfit to lead. However, lack of knowledge is not a barrier at Amazon; not having a big idea is. When you have one, your job is to write a Working Backwards document and give it to your manager. Basically, this is a press release from the day in the future your idea will be announced to the world. You're supposed to imagine it's a year or two later, turn around, and look backward to identify all the steps you took to get there. If approved, you then propose the Working Backwards doc to your leadership. At the first stage of the process, my document was just an idea detailed in a one-pager, neither validated nor accompanied by any proof-of-concept, which is perfectly acceptable. As it turned out, my boss's boss became my executive sponsor on it, so I proceeded to handpick an art director and design technologist from the London team and set about generating a prototype to demonstrate it. Next, I had to find someone really smart to help me. That's where the Phone Tool and goals came in.

The Phone Tool is the internal employee profile system with individuals' contact information, role, manager, badges of accomplishments, personal interests, and pretty much anything else Amazonians want to share about themselves. Because everyone has goals and programs, it's common to receive a call or email from a stranger looking for help, and that outreach is always, always honored. Every Amazonian is there for the same reason, all with high expectations placed upon them, representing every skillset and experience level under the sun. You learn quickly to lean on others to achieve your goals, and searching the Phone Tool for an expert in another field is a frequent activity. I found a director at A9, Amazon's search and advertising technology division, and emailed him at his offices in Palo Alto, California. "Hi. You don't know me," it read, "but my name is Steve and I'm executive creative director, international, based in the London office. I assume you have some aggressive goals this year, and I have an idea that might help you achieve them sooner." He wrote back as soon as he received it with "I'm listening."

That was December 2016, and by October of the following year, it was live and functional. Because the technology is patent-pending, I can't give you any more details than that, but suffice it to say, I learned that offering a stranger your assistance in achieving their goals is a powerful way to achieve your own, so long as they're complementary. That's a simple lesson I will employ not just wherever I work from now on but throughout my life. Even at the time of this writing, months after I left the company, that program is still alive, with new goals set for improving it. Goals and programs—turbo-charged by information-sharing between employees—is Amazon's special sauce. The company's ascendance is the direct result. Pretty straightforward.

PART IV

—

Loyalty

CHAPTER 10

Bonds

"Words are among our most precious possessions. With a promise, we give our word. Only by fulfilling it may we keep our word."

—UNCLE MILT

His soul wrenched all 24 hours of April 19, 1861. The letter was written, sealed, and stamped but remained on his desk. That week, colleagues and passersby saw his listless, grave countenance and wondered if he'd been stricken. Now he sat in his study in calm repose, ashen beneath gray hair and beard, rubbing his temples and appealing to God for an answer. Would he go or stay? Fight or abstain? It was almost too much for any man to bear.

Only 22 days earlier, Robert E. Lee swore an oath to the United States of America in accepting his promotion to colonel of the 1st Cavalry Regiment. He denounced secession as a betrayal of the Founding Fathers' efforts to realize a wondrous nation such as this, so Lee was on the side of the Unionists. "Mr. Blair," he wrote in a letter to presidential advisor Francis P. Blair, who'd recently offered him the position of major general to defend the US capital, "I look upon secession as anarchy. If I owned the four millions of slaves in the South, I would sacrifice them all to the Union; but how can I draw my sword upon Virginia, my native state?"

Lee's family members were by and large Unionists too, which made the decision so vexing. And after years on the battlefield, he understood firsthand the cruel horrors of war. Would he defend his state against the mighty armies of the North? Would he risk exposing his pro-Union sons to death on the side of the South? In the end, he would. He was loyal to the Commonwealth of Virginia. He was her son. Any honorable son defends his mother.

The next day, Lee mailed his resignation and, two days after that, made his way to the Virginia Convention in Richmond, where he was elected commander of Virginia state forces by 152 delegates, most of whom were also pro-Union, yet devoted to their state like Lee. As a symbolic gesture of his nomination, he was handed a sword that originally belonged to his wife's great grandfather George Washington, a fact that made it heavier still. Four years later, 620,000 Americans—approximately 2 percent of the national population—were dead.

LOYALTY: BATTLEFIELDS AND BRANDS

What is it about loyalty that compels people to make unimaginable sacrifices such as Lee's? We need merely look to Maslow's hierarchy of needs for our first clue. After the lowest two tiers, which feature requirements like food and shelter for survival, we find belonging. The need for relationships is in our nature because pulling together, sharing resources, and cooperating to protect the group was what kept early humans alive. Virginia wasn't a state to Robert E. Lee. It was the hub of all his relationships. Maybe Virginia was more than his mother. Perhaps it was *him*.

The human psyche evolved by developing cognitive systems designed to seek and secure support from other individuals, build loyalties and alliances, and assess the potential for advocacy from others in the group. Between alliances, threat-detection mechanisms were founded upon sensitivities to signals which helped us determine if the "other" is a danger to our group. On the right side of this deep-seated neuroprogramming is safety, trust, mutual progress, and loyalty; on the wrong side, fear, racism, xenophobia, and nationalism. Just look to the US Army, the setting where interracial relationships are among the most harmonious in America. The soldier of a different ethnic background, religion, or creed marching right next to you might just save your life one day.

In the brand space, the road to loyalty starts with trust or, put another way, avoiding the abuse of trust. For a brand or a person, that's a pretty low bar to clear. In the words of president and CEO of private equity firm Blackhawk Partners, Ziad K. Abdelnour, "Trust is earned, respect is given, and loyalty is demonstrated. Betrayal of any one of those is to lose all three." So just make a promise and keep it. That ought to be easy enough, right?

But not for brands. That's because customers don't even want to care about new brands in the first place. This defiance is inbuilt too, as neurochemical passageways are set as a default to detect threats of all sizes, not just physical harm but of wasting time or money—even just having to deal with confusion or making a choice. It seems we are hardwired to start with "no" until external stimuli motivate us out of our reluctance. In his book *Resistance and Persuasion*, Dr. Eric Knowles breaks this resistance down to three types: reactance, which is resistance to the persuasion process itself; skepticism, the resistance directed against the offer or proposal; and inertia, or reluctance to change. That's a high wall to climb for brands, so your pitch better be immediate and effective, or likelihood is low you'll get another chance. This is what makes positive word of mouth so important to marketers everywhere. When a loved one with your interests in mind recommends a product to fulfill a need you've expressed, most of your resistance goes out the window. The endorser's reputation (trust) with you is on the line, so the advice is received with a strong "group safety" response already implied.

IT'S ALL CHEMICAL, REALLY

The whole dynamic is of course physiological. Dopamine is a neurotransmitter synthesized by the brain to send signals of a pending reward from neurons to other nerve cells. The substance is also stimulated by unpredictability and small bits of information, and it's important for a wide array of brain functions like thinking, mood, and sleep. Contrary to its popular characterization as the "pleasure drug," pharmacologists believe that dopamine is the chemical of *incentive*, or what drives an organism toward a desired outcome. The second chemical, oxytocin, a.k.a., the "hug drug" is a hormone secreted by the brain during social bonding, sex, childbirth, bonding with a baby, and breastmilk production. It is the stimulant of trust, the glue that bonds families and communities, the grease in the wheels of belonging.

Both of these powerful substances are critical to human decision-making. It appears that there's something biological to Maslow's belonging after all. Not long after the inflection point of 2007, press coverage of these technologies' effects on our brains started to pour out (and hasn't stopped). In 2010, Adam Penenberg of *Fast Company* put himself inside an MRI to have his neurohormonal releases measured every second while engaging with, among other things, Twitter. The result: his oxytocin levels spiked 13.2 percent within ten minutes, which is equivalent to a groom on his wedding day, the article claimed.

In 2017, David Brooks told us in a *New York Times* op-ed titled "How Evil is Tech?" that "tech companies understand what causes dopamine surges in the brain and they lace their products with 'hijacking techniques' that lure us in and create 'compulsion loops.'" As I mentioned above, dopamine is released when someone encounters unpredictability and small bits of information, and acts as motivator toward a reward. Oxytocin is generated when one bonds with another. Combined, they seem perfectly predisposed to social media to me and may as well be board members at Facebook/Instagram, Twitter, and Snap. They're fully responsible for the semi-addicted states of millions of people around the world at any given moment and, as such, fuel the attention economy.

AFFINITY OR ADDICTION?

Brands want in on the dependence action too. Is it possible to get as hooked on a mental story as a teenager is to Instagram? It appears so. In June 2018, the *Huffington Post* listed some of the most "outrageous baby names of 2017," which included brands Tesla (130 girls, 11 boys), Fanta (24 girls), and Maybelline (20 girls). Twelve girls and six boys were named Espn after the cable sports network. Of course, names can be changed rather easily later in life, so is there a more enduring honor a brand can earn? Ask Harley-Davidson, Apple, and Nike, whose logos are permanently inked onto their fans' hides in tattoo parlors everywhere each year.

Naming kids after an electric car company and staining your bicep with the Harley eagle aren't just extreme acts of brand love, they're tickets to a different kind of social network that doesn't require web access. For the same reason people put bumper stickers on their cars touting their political affiliations, broadcasting one's brand addiction admits him to an exclusive club of devotees who tell the world, "I love Brand X so much more than you do." It also binds the club member's life aspirations to the brand's ideals. Etch the Nike swoosh on your left pectoral, and you're communicating your athletic prowess. Name your baby girl Chanel, and you've told the world you want her to grow up to be stylish and live a life of luxury. Marketers are starting to learn how to activate dopamine and oxytocin by encouraging such behavior. CEO of gym chain Anytime Fitness, Chuck Runyon, offers full reimbursement to anyone who gets Anytime's "Running Man" logo tattooed on their bodies and sends him a photo with an explanation of why they did it. He calls it "ROEI," or Return on Emotional Investment.

TEAM FIRST

Sports teams are brands just as much as sports networks, and their legions of fanatics have been naming kids after superstars and ordering up tattoos of their logos and even championship dates for decades. As mentioned earlier, I've lived on both sides of the Atlantic, and my love for English Premier League Football started when I attended my first match in London in 1996. But it wasn't until I lived there that I saw loyalty in its most unabashed form.

My favorite pastime in the world, far and away, is college football, which inspires a fervor here in the States that collectively dwarfs the NFL. The pageantry and reliable sellouts of stadiums holding 100,000-plus fans every fall Saturday across the country is a permanent fixture of the American landscape. The English, on the other hand, take it to a level that's hard to explain unless you've witnessed it live—to the point that the supporters of each side are forbidden to associate with each other once on the grounds, enter the stadium together, or even sit next to one another to prevent grievous violence and rioting. I once brought my friend to a West Ham home match (that's my team) versus Brighton & Hove Albion (his), and naturally bought a pair of tickets together. What a dumb Yank rookie move that was. If a fan of the away team is seen cheering for his side in the area of the stadium reserved for home fans, event security staff will immediately rush to escort him off the premises for his own protection. So while we got thumped 3-nil, my friend couldn't cheer or even show his excitement. He'd just hit my thigh with the back of his hand 100 times a minute until play resumed. Lots of dopamine for him. Oxytocin for me? Yeah, no.

It's easy, then, to see where many of our loyalties derive. Keyword: "where." Fervent followers of college football, just as those of the World Cup and Olympics, adhere to the same archetype. The performance of athletes competing in these events under "our" flag is a powerful indictment of where we fans are from—precisely as in Robert E. Lee's case—and we will go to great ends to see our side to victory, for it paints us from "here" in a superior light to them from "there." Just ask a priest what demand exists for marriage ceremonies in any major college football town on fall Saturdays, and my point will be made.

As such, team loyalty is prone to exploitation by team ownership. According to statistics portal Statista, the price of the average ticket to a National Football League game increased 60.7 percent, from $62.38 to $100.26, between 2006 and 2018. Ask yourself: did the quality of the League's product on the field rise 60 percent during that period, the $10 hot dogs reduce to $4, the restroom lines get 60 percent shorter? Hardly. All of that in the face of the NFL's TV contracts, which totaled $6 billion in 2016 and are projected at a few billion more today. How can they justify this? Because loyalty, that's why. We pay gladly for the dopamine high the anticipation of a win gives us, and the oxytocin of hugging fellow fans when our team pulls off the victory.

Off the field, combining two high-loyalty brands together can create a result much, much larger than the sum of its parts. Exhibit A: Nike's collaboration with Kanye West. In 2007, the rapper/business mogul began development of a shoe line with the brand's creative director Mark Smith. It was the first time a nonathlete would codesign a shoe at Nike, the world's largest sports apparel and equipment manufacturer. The Air Yeezy shoes launched in 2009 to immediate popularity and intentional scarcity, yielding prices upwards of $10,000 a pair on the aftermarket. The same thing happened three years later with the release of the Air Yeezy II. While I laughed about these sneakerheads paying such astronomical prices, it proves my point that combining two loyalty heavyweights can produce an astonishing effect for the right audience. I'm hardly immune. The moment I learned one of my favorite footwear brands, Dr. Martens, collaborated with one of my favorite bands, Joy Division, on a limited-edition boot line, I couldn't run to the store fast enough. We are dopes for dopamine.

WHAT'S IT ALL MEAN TO YOU?

Chances are your brand doesn't attract legions of disciples like a trendy shoe company or a hip-hop artist can, but that doesn't mean you shouldn't consider collaborating with another brand (whether that's a company or a person) also loved by your best customers. If you're listening to them as often and intently as you should be, you probably know what or whom that might be right off the top of your head. If not, ask them. To that end, if you haven't already, find your brand's biggest enthusiasts and establish an exclusive community for them. Reward them for their loyalty, nominate one every three months to "brand expert" status for special perks, and tap into them constantly.

Earlier, I wrote that money is the most popular currency and information the most powerful. Loyalty then is the amplifier currency. If you can find a way to combine it with any of the other three—the backbone of any respectable loyalty rewards program—you'll enjoy a high return on that investment. When it's done right, I call it "joyalty," because of the brain chemicals released in the recipient. That's what a great brand can elicit.

Finally, loyalty is, like marriage, a vow. And as partners in the longest-lasting marriages know, the promise made on wedding day has to be remade every single morning to handle the inevitable ups and downs endemic to any relationship. Customer devotion is not a "set it and forget it" mentality. Remember, they're at the controls, and they have every right to be promiscuous. Have meaningful conversations daily about the next way you plan to stimulate dopamine and oxytocin production in your customer. Give them real reasons to say, "I do," every time you propose.

CHAPTER 11

Loyalty and the Customer

"Real loyalty has a shape. It's full-circle."

—UNCLE MILT

"Just two more days to go," the man in front of her said as he awoke, rolled over on his side, and adjusted his sleeping bag on the sidewalk.

"I just pray it doesn't rain," she responded, rolling her coffee cup back and forth in her palms as she looked at up at the morning sky.

The four 20-something bros behind her did not sleep the entire night, preferring instead to channel their nervous energy into a spirited match of Euchre. The card game prompted shouts and curses from its participants all night, depriving her of anything close to one uninterrupted hour of rest. She rubbed the bags under her eyes and pinched the bridge of her nose. Two more days.

The day was Wednesday, June 27, 2007; the location, Fifth Avenue in Midtown Manhattan opposite Central Park. Formed only the day before, the human queue already snaked for blocks. The man ahead of the woman in line was a 54-year-old marketing executive. She was half his age and a web designer. Both were dressed in high-end athletic wear and surrounded by performance camping gear. Most of the people in line could be described this way, so the scene could hardly be confused for a gathering of homeless so common to New York's underbelly. What then could this be?

Five months earlier, Steve Jobs announced his company's intentions to move into the mobile phone business, and a frenzy ensued. After a barrage of unprecedented hype, the iPhone would be launched that Friday, and everyone in attendance would be rewarded for their single-mindedness with the right to plunk $499 or $599 down for a new device called the iPhone. The product would go on to change the telecommunications world and contribute mightily to Apple's market cap, which became the first to top $1 trillion in 2018.

In the context of brand currency, these customers were spending the sizable sum of loyalty they'd saved up for Apple over the previous decades. Hundreds of well-heeled professional adults slept on sidewalks for three days on a promise that their mental stories about Apple would continue in the same, or perhaps even more positive, trajectory after acquiring this black shingle comprised of metal, transistors, and glass. Years later, in the 2011 BBC documentary *Secrets of the Superbrands*, neuroscientists compared MRI results of Apple fans' brains to those of people who consider themselves "very religious" and discovered that Apple and religion stimulate the same reaction in the same part of the brain. On that day, then, we'd have been within our rights to consider the throng a procession and the Apple Store its cathedral. That's a lot of dopamine.

Can you imagine the consequences if the iPhone flopped? The most loyal Apple evangelists sacrificed their own personal comfort and vacation days from work on what basically amounted to a bet. All of that loyalty spent on a rotten product would have taken years for Apple to earn back. Thankfully for Jobs and company, the iPhone was the sensation they assured, and the rest is now the subject of business books and an armored truck dumping more than $200 million on Apple's bottom line every year.

While only a handful of brands reach Apple's rarified air, every brand owner should keep top of mind the other side of the loyalty coin, forgiveness. Companies and the mental stories they generate are owned and managed by people, after all, and people make mistakes. Most gaffes, like Amazon's

Fire Phone, are made with the best intentions but somehow miss the mark. Amazon's loyalty balance may have a taken a hit, but it was short-lived and customers moved on. The loyalty they'd stockpiled in the brand made quick work of that issue. (A former colleague of mine swears Bezos did it on purpose to show the world that Amazon was willing to take risks, but I digress.) Other, more systemic mistakes, like not listening intently to your customers or investing in customer service, almost come off feeling intentional—or at least willfully ignorant—to the audience and can sound the death knell for any brand in time. This seems to be the bugaboo of the telecom and cable TV industries, which routinely score lowest in overall customer satisfaction.

THE LOYALTY BANK: DEBITS AND CREDITS

So there are mistakes, and yeah, we all make them. Then there are disasters. While this book is dedicated to branding in the now, I'd be remiss if I didn't include perhaps the most famous example of all time, which took place in the fall of 1982, when Chicagoland residents started dropping dead after taking cyanide-laced Tylenol capsules. In a matter of days, seven victims fell prey to the original poisonings, and when autopsies linked them all to both the deadly chemical and Tylenol ingestion, every brand's worst nightmare had come true. Warnings were issued across the country in every mass medium possible as police patrols cruised greater Chicago with loudspeakers shouting advisories to cease usage of the pain reliever.

In a masterstroke of public relations worthy of featuring in university PR books (I studied it in my Public Relations 101 course at school), Johnson & Johnson didn't shrink from its responsibilities but rather stopped all production of the product and issued its own warnings to the public, hospitals, and distributors. Within one week, it initiated a nationwide recall, taking out of circulation some 31 million bottles of Tylenol products. After thorough inspection, Johnson & Johnson was cleared of any responsibility for the deaths— in fact, the company was lauded for its transparency and rapid response—but severe damage had been done to entire consumer product sectors, which, after more copycat killings around the country, would be forced to introduce tamper-resistant packaging and other expensive safety measures to their quality control methods.

A culprit was never identified, but if whoever he or she was wanted to kill both people and the brand, they failed in the latter. Before the scare, Tylenol enjoyed 35 percent of the over-the-counter pain reliever market; a few weeks after the murders, it plummeted to just 8 percent. Within a year and after investing $100 million, it rebounded and resumed the top spot, but it's hard to believe most brands could have withstood such an ordeal. The forgiveness that Tylenol was able to draw from its customers' bank of loyalty points ultimately saved the division.

When an estimated 1.5 million Thomas the Tank Engine toys were recalled in 2007 for containing lead paint, manufacturer RC2 Corporation did not heed Tylenol's lesson, at least initially. The company first asked customers to mail back the toys at their own expense, infuriating parents and firing up an angry press, who were left to write headlines like the *New York Times*'s "RC2 Train Wreck" when corporate leadership did not return repeated calls. After reaching a $1.25 million settlement with the Consumer Product Safety Commission (CPSC) and overhauling its inspection process, Thomas has earned its way back to being among the most enduring toy brands.

The prior two instances—one a criminal act which just happened to involve a particular brand, and the other, surfacing the perils of manufacturing in China where lax consumer product health standards require extreme levels of scrutiny when products arrive in the US—were limited to one instance and aren't indicative of trends at either company. Chipotle Mexican Grill, unfortunately, can't catch a break—or an outbreak, to be more accurate. In September 2015, the first of many foodborne illness outbreaks took place in Minnesota, where 45 cases of salmonella were reported. A month later, the chain was forced to close 43 restaurants in Washington and Oregon after an E. coli epidemic. By November, California,

New York, and Ohio joined the list. Two months after that, a Chipotle in Massachusetts was closed after an unrelated norovirus contamination sent 120 Boston College students to the hospital, at which point co-CEO and cofounder Steve Ells visited *The Today Show* to personally apologize to the American public. Just 10 days after that appearance, E. coli was again reported at stores in Oklahoma, Kansas, and North Dakota. Of course, shares in the company toppled and same-store sales took a nosedive, but somehow, the brand carried on.

Amidst all this, in a moment worthy of a veritable Algonquin Round Table, executives cited bad in-store experiences like long lines and dirty dining areas as the reasons behind poor sales. In January 2016, Ells said he was "extremely confident" that the chain's food-safety crisis was over. It wasn't. In July 2017, a franchise in Sterling, Virginia, was shuttered temporarily due to another norovirus outbreak, forcing the company's hand to replace Ells, who'd been at the helm of the chain for more than two decades. Shortly thereafter, IWasPoisoned.com, a website customers can use to self-report foodborne illness, showed a report count of 29 per 100 stores for August, September, and October of that year. In second place sat Taco Bell with five reports.

While I am absolutely certain that Ells meant every word of his apologies, his talk ultimately proved too cheap. In February 2018, UBS analyst Dennis Geiger, in partnership with the UBS Evidence Lab, analyzed online customer review ratings and found that the company's reputation was even lower than at the height of its 2015 and 2016 outbreaks. In the study, Geiger reported 37 percent of the more than 1,600 customers polled online claimed "food safety concerns" as their primary reason for avoiding Chipotle, compared to roughly 15 percent for McDonald's in the same category.

A second Ohio outbreak in 2018 has me wondering how much longer this can go on. Surely, even the almighty burrito has only so much customer loyalty in the bank. We all know that Americans have crazily short memories, but how many more people have to get sick before the brand itself falls ill and ultimately passes away? "Chipotle is a case study in what happens when a brand loses the trust of its consumers," David Henkes, principal at food service industry research firm Technomic, told CNBC in February 2018. "The market is too competitive right now, and consumers have so many choices, that once that bond is broken, it's hard to get consumers back."

LOYALTY AS AN ATM

For brands that don't need to rely on the currency for mistake-forgiveness, loyalty is a powerful revenue-driver when releasing new products. If you like your Samsung phone, you might consider a Samsung TV when you're in-market. This is known in marketing as the "halo effect," and it's one of the drivers behind the success of companies like Amazon and Apple, which have wandered far away from their original core offerings, books and desktop computers respectively, over the past few decades. If I like shopping at Amazon, I'll sign up for Prime. If that service exceeds my expectations, I'll consider the Fire TV when I cut myself off of cable and get an over-the-top (OTT) streaming box. However, it can backfire. Extend too far away from your brand's sweet spot in search of more revenue, create a bad customer experience, and you'll come off as an abuser of loyalty. This places a premium on making sure every single touchpoint is one of consistently high quality so trust is first preserved and then increased.

Since loyalty is a currency, it flows both ways. Customers receive from brands as well as spend on them. *Harvard Business Review* tells us that the cost to acquire a new customer is five to 25 times higher than keeping a current one, and that increasing retention rates by just 5 percent increases profits by 25 to 95 percent. Little things that don't cost a company much can go far in the world of rewarding a customer for her business.

A great place to start is the currency of time. A dedicated line at a check-in/checkout counter accessible by loyalty program members, for example, sends a clear message of value. I absolutely love this at the airline, hotel, and rental car programs I've joined. Remember, loyalty is the amplifier currency, so multiplying it with saving the customer's time has an oversized effect in the dopamine department, and it costs far, far less than trying to win a new customer. Other perks like free downloads and birthday discounts are also inexpensive ways to say thanks and build up that loyalty level, which you're going to need as an insurance policy the next time you screw up (and you will). But that's only after you've invested heavily in the blocking and tackling of loyalty—customer service (a.k.a., the new marketing) and listening. Finally, if you're using only churn rate, or amount of customers you've lost per unit of time, to determine the health of your customer loyalty, recognize that you're usually at least six months behind the time you started disappointing those customers. This is why it's known as a "lagging indicator," meaning you're only looking backward and wholly unable to be proactive, only reactive.

Amazon doesn't have a loyalty rewards program, yet most people aren't surprised when it routinely tops brand loyalty surveys. As a new Amazonian, I asked my boss why Amazon doesn't have such an offering, to which he responded, "Amazon *is* a loyalty program." This told me that LPs, goals, programs, customer service in all its forms, and a total commitment to fulfilling promises is what it takes, not necessarily miles or points. You can't buy your way the top of the loyalty mountain. And inside Amazon, landing the number one spot on a brand equity or trust survey was rarely observed or even discussed. When every conversation, every hire, every action is done on behalf of the customer, then only total success is the expectation. I saw this akin to Hall of Fame Detroit Lions running back Barry Sanders, who calmly handed the ball to the referee after scoring one of his 1,991 touchdowns and never, ever celebrated. Hold aggressively high intentions for your performance and, once they're fulfilled, act like you've been there before and move on to the next TD.

WHAT'S IT ALL MEAN TO YOU?

Customer loyalty takes years to build and a moment to lose. Consumers have so much choice in a marketplace where every player is jockeying for their dollar, and they don't owe you a second chance. Where you work, is the customer experience the first thing on the meeting agenda, or does it start with the bottom line and pleasing the shareholders? Is loyalty a "first dollar in" notion or does it sit somewhere behind legal and lobbying? Try this: listen closely to the verb tenses people use when discussing priorities. Is it past (reactive) or future (proactive) tense? Next, listen for the "person" pronouns your colleagues use in important business discussions. Is it first-person plural (we) or third-person plural (they)? This will give you an idea of where your brand stands with respect to your customer and how far it has to go to find the holy grail.

CHAPTER 12

——

Loyalty and the Brand

"Brands can learn so much from a dog—honesty and loyalty for starters."

—UNCLE MILT

One by one, the 23 South Korean men dressed in business-casual solemnly approached the stage as the crowd watched with bated breath. It was cold in Shijiazhuang, northern China, in November 2016, but it was about to get colder for the visitors from Seoul. In single file, each of the executives mounted the platform, took their positions, turned to the audience, and knelt down on both knees. They knelt so far down that their heads touched the ground. They held the position for five long seconds.

The room met the gesture—intended to demonstrate apology and gratitude—with equal parts light clapping and awkward gasps. The Samsung execs did not mean to offend their hosts, dozens of Samsung distributors, with their actions. Even after it was discovered that 92 Galaxy Note 7 smartphones were shipped with batteries prone to overheating (some of which caught fire in the US), and then Samsung recalled the 2.5 million devices it had shipped around the world, these distributors stuck with the brand and remarkably placed more orders during the event, humbling the executives deeply. In Korea, kneeling in this manner is honored as a show of thanks, sorrow, and deference. Not so in China, where the public was outraged by what it saw as corporate officials pandering to the crowd. In that country, kneeling is reserved for pious moments of prayer in a temple, showing respect for elders, and even begging for food. The accidental cultural misappropriation set off a social media firestorm. The Chinese were incensed. Poor Samsung just couldn't win. Its market value plummeted $14.3 billion as the device faced an airline ban and the company settled personal injury lawsuits. And now this.

Like Tylenol and Thomas the Tank Engine, Samsung would rebound a year later after the successful launches of the flame-free Galaxy S8 and Note 9, earning back the trust they enjoyed before the crisis. The brand had apparently built up enough loyalty for millions of customers worldwide to give them another chance. If the Galaxy Note 7 were their first-ever phone, it likely would have been game over for at least that product division. But this was an aberration in their history. They apologized, fixed the problem, and weathered the storm.

Rapid and full mistake-admission is inherently a Day 1 attitude, and it can save a company. Or a hockey team. While I've known Torontonians who would sooner part with a limb than their Maple Leafs tickets, the 2011–2012 season was a particularly bad one. After an epic collapse at the end of the season, which included four shutouts in their final ten games, the Leafs finished under .500 and missed the playoffs for the seventh straight year. Bad for any team but unacceptable to an original-six club with unfailing home-rink sellouts. This time, things were different with the fans, whose frustration turned to outright anger—pretty difficult to achieve with Canadians, who may just be the coolest-headed race on the planet. Sensing this palpable displeasure (and assuming the role as the butt of other NHL markets' jokes), management took out a full-page apology in the *Toronto Star* and other area dailies that read, "We have fallen short of everyone's expectations, and for that we are sorry. We take full responsibility for how this team performs on the ice and we make no excuses." In other words, they invested some of the loyalty they'd earned over 95 seasons to soften the blow. The next year, Toronto finished the strike-shortened season with a winning record of 26–17–5 and made the Stanley Cup Playoffs. At least in this case, it seems that publicly owning up to your failures can save your fan base and even increase quality.

SOLUTIONS, NOT EXCUSES

As I wrote earlier, one of the Amazon LPs, Earn Trust, places the expectation on employees to be "vocally self-critical." This has woven an innate spirit of "we all drop the ball every once in a while, so as long as it was truly in pursuit of improving the customer experience, you don't make the same mistake again, and you share it out so that others don't either, all is forgiven." Thankfully I've never been on the receiving end of one of Bezos's forwarded emails containing only a "?" in the body. It's not a death sentence, but if you get enough of them from the boss, let's just say that can't be good. While not the dread question mark, my manager once got an email forwarded from his boss who received it from the team monitoring customer ad feedback. I later learned from a West Coast counterpart that a customer who led a church choir—which used ad-supported Fire Tablets as their songbooks—had written us about a full-screen ad for a TV show featuring an actress bearing a little too much skin for their liking. When they activated the devices that morning in their house of worship, it offended them enough to warrant an email expressing their disappointment. The team who built it set about immediately pausing, rectifying, and retrafficking the campaign, and a valuable lesson was learned.

After ADX changed the imagery, our management gave us all a crash course in the "Andon cord" and instructed us to "pull" it whenever we see something that might go out the door and confuse, frustrate, annoy, insult, shout at, or frighten a customer of any age. Generally credited to W. Edwards Deming, the Iowan engineer and management consultant who helped steer Japan's post–World War II industrial rebirth, Andon is a quality-assurance methodology first employed by Toyota that enables every frontline worker to stop the production line by pulling an overhead cord after discovering a quality concern or defect. Doing so would activate an *andon*, Japanese for "lantern," to direct management to the location of the problem. While every division at Amazon has its own version of the Andon cord, it got its start in the fulfillment centers, where thousands of parcels moving at high speeds can have huge ramifications on shipping times if a snag occurs, causing a massive parcel pileup. At ADX, stopping the entire operation and calling leads in to evaluate would be a mandate from that day forward. The cost of upsetting one advertiser was less than zero compared to customers in a church choir.

Amazon calls the mechanism by which one publicizes errors to prevent others from making the same mistake a "COE," or Correction of Error document. This is not a finger-pointing exercise; rather, it is understood across the company that mistakes are the price of innovation, so unless there was real negligence involved, a COE isn't a pink slip for the writer or those mentioned in it. I wrote one a few years in, not (thankfully) because I myself made an error, but because my team was one of many parties involved in a campaign utilizing code we'd never deployed before, which effectively paralyzed the pages the ads were on, so my boss thought it'd be a good experience for me.

While the error is underway, Amazonians employ a four-step process to stop and resolve it: Identification, Mitigation, Correction, and Understanding. After the fourth step, the COE is generated, which details the chronology and ownership of the issue, as well as steps to prevent its recurrence.

My favorite part of the COE is "5 Whys," an interrogation technique invented by the founder of Toyota Industries (*again* with the Toyota) used to arrive at an error's root cause. We start with the problem statement and then ask "why?" five times. For example: "My mobile phone can't make outgoing calls. Why? Because I'm not getting service. Why? Because my service was turned off. Why? Because I didn't pay my bill. Why? Because I'm out of money. Why? Because I spent everything I have on lottery tickets and didn't win." Resembling a conversation with your average two-year-old, I'll bet that if you try this the next time something unanticipated strikes your business, you might be surprised where the 5 Whys takes you. If a colleague were to tell you, "My phone can't make calls," would you have honestly concluded her financial irresponsibility was to blame? You'd probably have initially gone with "it must be in airplane mode." I learned in writing the COE that our first inclinations about problems are seldom correct.

ALWAYS ROOM FOR IMPROVEMENT

When it comes to brands spending loyalty to overcome a setback with its customers, this is the sound of me calling a spade a spade. Amazon could stand to walk the walk even better by behaving outwardly more like the way it does internally. For most of its mistakes, they react swiftly and honestly, but not everywhere—at least as interpreted by the majority of customers I've spoken to. Despite some tangibly positive actions recently, there's some hangover.

The first is the taxation perception issue I mentioned earlier. Because Amazon operates legally and pays what it's told by the governments whose jurisdictions its facilities call home, I don't feel an apology is warranted per se. However, I do think leadership would do itself a favor by at least responding to negative coverage with justification details that everyday people can understand. The second perception problem is its employee satisfaction record, primarily in the fulfillment centers, where strikes have been called in Europe. On Prime Day 2018, the biggest shopping day in its history, workers in Germany, Spain, and Poland walked off the job in protest of unhealthy working conditions. The contrast between Bezos's wealth and their wages was not lost on these employees, but by October 2018, their actions appear to have paid off when Bezos said in a statement, "We listened to our critics, thought hard about what we wanted to do, and decided we want to lead. We're excited about this change and encourage our competitors and other large employers to join us."

Amazon then raised the minimum wage to $15 an hour in the US, £9.50 in the UK, and elsewhere. I was impressed.

Finally, the August 15, 2015, exposé printed in the *New York Times* under the headline "Wrestling Big Ideas in a Bruising Workplace" shed light on many current and former employees' awful experiences. I can tell you without hesitation that Amazon leadership took this report extremely seriously and asked every employee who'd witnessed or been the brunt of this behavior to come to HR and report it. Not long after, they implemented measures like paternity leave and extended maternity leave, and introduced a new performance review process. Those were loyalty investments that rapidly made a difference.

One considerably more damning case study that's still playing out at the time of this writing is the Volkswagen diesel emissions scandal. In 2014, the California Air Resources Board (CARB) commissioned research on the diesel-emissions discrepancies between American and European vehicles. One of the three data-collection sources CARB contracted was West Virginia University's Center for Alternative Fuels, Engines, and Emissions. During their research, they drove around Los Angeles analyzing exhaust from the tailpipes of two VWs, but for some reason, the data they captured kept coming up wrong. The Chassis Dynamometers they'd custom-engineered for in-use testing (i.e., not on a stationary rig in a laboratory but out on the road) was showing pollutants at a thousand times what they'd seen in the lab. "This can't be right," they assumed, but continued to capture and crunch the data for evaluation nonetheless.

After a year of analysis, the truth that slowly emerged would shock the corporate world and VW fans everywhere. Volkswagen had indeed installed "defeat" software in its vehicles that detected when they were being tested in a lab and instantly cut emissions to legal levels. The world's largest automaker never expected its automobiles to be tested on the road and so didn't see it coming. Unbeknownst to them, West Virginia researchers had built their Chassis Dynamometers to be delivered to projects analyzing many heavy-duty vehicles, not the other way around as is the industry standard. WVU didn't raise the alarm to the US Environmental Protection Agency of their findings but rather, to VW's bitter chagrin, the International Council on Clean Transportation which had funded CARB's research. After months of denial, VW knew it was busted and in January 2017 plead guilty to rigging 11 million vehicles, leading to the resignation and arrest of Volkswagen Group CEO Martin Winterkorn and many other execs for turning a blind eye to the manipulation, attempting to defraud the US, and conspiracy to violate the Clean Air Act. The German corporation would later be slapped with $4.3 billion in penalties and more than $10 billion in lawsuits from investors and customers.

Years of loyalty squandered overnight. VW taken down by

WVU. This story just has to be a movie someday. Of course, it could have all been avoided if the company fostered a Day 1 environment where mistakes—in this case, missing the 2009 deadline to meet the new emission standards in the US—were begrudgingly accepted if everyone involved were genuinely doing their best by the customer. Yes, VW would've taken a big financial punch below the belt in the short term and a tongue-lashing from shareholders, but nothing like they're facing now. As Andreas Tilp, legal counsel for the lead plaintiff, told the court, "VW knew by 2008 that they wouldn't be able to meet US pollution standards. They should have told everybody, 'We won't make it.'" Instead, they placed a bet that no one would notice and lost, earning them the title of Lance Armstrong of auto brands and two consecutive 9 percent drops in Interbrand's Best Global Brand Rankings 2015 and 2016 (after moving up 23 percent from 2013 to 2014).

Before the scandal, VW was more like Subaru, which nabbed the number two spot in the 2018 Edmunds Trade-In Loyalty Report that tracks vehicles traded in for the same brand. The little Japanese carmaker-that-could demonstrated consistency and quality sufficiently to see its loyalty jump 45 percent during the prior decade. Brands like Subaru receive the loyalty currency from their customers in the form of not just repeat purchases but offline word of mouth (WOM) and online social media likes, follows, and shares. In 2016, Subaru's WOM scored at the top of the industry alongside lux brands like Ferrari and Porsche, according to a report from analytics firm Engagement Labs. Its commitment to sustainability and durability shines through everything they do, and customers love it. A Day 1 approach has the power to make your brand the loveable tree-hugger among the deceitful emissions-scammers.

SELLING SOMETHING? GREAT—NOW WHAT'S YOUR PURPOSE?

WOM from real customers is the new celebrity testimonial, which is why social posts touting a brand's strengths litter TV commercials. Knowing this, brands have been asserting their ideals and stepping up their cause marketing game to an estimated $2.14 billion in 2018, a projected increase of 4.4 percent over 2017, according to an ESP Sponsorship Report. Furthermore, as 2018 Shelton Group's "Brands & Stands: Social Purpose is the New Black" study tells us, "86 percent of consumers believe that companies should take a stand for social issues and 64 percent of those who said it's 'extremely important' for a company to take a stand on a social issue said they were 'very likely' to purchase a product based on that commitment." This is expected to increase as the next generation of consumers comes of age. Per the 2018 Survey of Young People and Social Change, "76 percent of young people said they have purchased (53 percent) or would consider purchasing (23 percent) a brand/product to show support for the issues the brand supported." TOMS Shoes, Bomba socks, and FIGS medical scrubs, with their "buy a pair, give a pair" model, were built from the ground up on this philosophy, and they've become really successful. (Admittedly, they do take some stick for essentially killing the shoe, sock, and scrubs industries in the developing countries which receive their donations.) The results are clear: knowing where your brand stands on social issues and supporting causes which align to that position is smart business.

Social responsibility plays such an important role to brand health today that some marketers have come to see it as the new loyalty rewards program. And if you can find a way to cleverly combine them both, you're really filling your loyalty vault. This is well understood by Cincinnati-based grocery chain Kroger, whose Community Rewards program doles out millions each year to schools, churches, and other nonprofits when customers swipe their Plus Card at checkout, earning them rewards points in the process.

Digital has helped industry-leading loyalty programs like Starbucks Rewards come a long way from the days when American Airlines launched the first modern loyalty rewards program, AAdvantage, in 1981. While groundbreaking, the concept of incentivizing repeat purchase entered the American retail lexicon as long ago as the 1700s, when shop owners gave customers copper tokens that could be redeemed for price breaks on future purchases. With the Starbucks app, customers track their rewards, get special offers, order ahead of arrival (which helps reduce all customers' in-store waiting), and pay—but more importantly for the brand, generate immense amounts of location-based data. At the end of 2017, Starbucks stated that mobile payments accounted for 30 percent of all transactions. Everybody wins. A friend of mine recently went on a cruise. Onboard were a dozen coffee shops that were mostly desolate except for the one Starbucks location, which saw lines of app-using customers flowing out well into the hallway. Along with implementing corrective actions, taking responsibility, and apologizing, it's this type of loyalty that helps a brand overcome an ugly incident like the one that took place at a Philadelphia location in May 2018, when a manager had two African American men arrested for sitting at a table but not ordering anything. Convenience and consistency make money, sure, but in times of need they can be called upon to make up for blunders.

Convincing someone to not just try your brand once but to come back again—and even evangelize it—is more challenging than ever. Like a broken record, I've repeated that choice abounds and errors are inevitable. To succeed, brand owners must learn to be comfortable in the uncomfortable role of second fiddle, instantly owning every miscue, remaining transparent, and keeping the conversation going with the customer as long as she wants to have it (but not a moment longer). For this to be possible, we must hire humble people and coach modesty constantly, even promoting and terminating staffers against it. In the age of assistance, arrogance hardly breeds loyalty. When in doubt, just channel your inner Rafael Nadal. In a 2011 interview, the Spanish tennis icon was asked why he flies economy, to which he responded that his iPod sounded the same in coach as in first class. Frugality, humility, and 17 majors to boot.

PART V

—

Time

CHAPTER 13

———

Breaths

"But for friction does the past become the future."

—UNCLE MILT

Albert Einstein was angry. As the object of his ire, the post-man, ambled away from his home after dropping the mail through the slot, he cursed under his breath and surveyed the correspondence cluttering his foyer. Today's was an especially large haul, even by his standards. Fourteen years earlier, between March and June of 1905, Einstein wrote four papers that would launch his voyage into history. The first examined how to measure the size of molecules in a liquid; the second, how to assess their movement; the third concentrated on how light travels in packets called "photons"; and the fourth, an introduction to special relativity. Then, a few months after those theses, in what seemed like an "Oh, and one more thing" afterthought, he issued a fifth paper claiming that matter and energy were interchangeable at the atomic level, that $E = MC^2$, forming the scientific foundation of nuclear energy.

A few hundred years before, Galileo Galilei established the classic version of relativity by first asking the reader to imagine himself standing on a dock, watching a ship moving steadily across his field of vision. Next, he should think of a sailor atop the ship's mast dropping a rock. Would it land at the base of the mast or a short distance back from the mast—the length the ship moved while the rock was falling? From the sailor's perspective, the rock fell straight down. From the dock, the rock appeared to descend on a slight slope, traveling a marginally longer distance than a straight line. Both you and the sailor would be right. The path of the rock is relative to the observer.

With one simple update to Galileo's scenario, Einstein would change the world. What if it were not a rock that is sent toward the ship's deck but a beam of light? One evening, he walked home from his job at the patent office in Bern, Switzerland, discussing the problem with friend and fellow physicist Michele Besso. Suppose the mast is 186,282 miles high, the distance that light travels per second in a vacuum. Knowing that the speed of light is constant, as opposed to the rock, which accelerates due to gravity, it suddenly struck the 26-year-old that if he applied the same principle, and you change the distance the light has traveled in one second, you must also change the time. *Change the time?*

He called that theory "special relativity," or the relationship between a body at rest and another moving at a constant velocity. When he advanced the concept to apply to bodies moving at changing velocities two years later, he called it "general relativity." Daydreaming these scenarios, while important to scientific progress for centuries, was the easy part. It would take another eight years to work out the math to support them.

By the time he did, he was a professor at the University of Berlin. World War I had broken out and Western Europe was on the path to ruin. For Einstein's work to reach the wider academic and scientific worlds, he would have to sneak over enemy lines with his writings to a friend in Holland who forwarded them to Arthur Eddington in England, one of the few men who could put them to the test. If his theories were correct, a solar eclipse would offer the perfect opportunity to observe gravity's effect on light, but the next one was a few years away. That was a good thing at the time, however. No one would be able to prioritize theories about light, gravity, and time with the world at war.

Armistice Day in November 1918 put an end to all that. Compelled by the considerable clout of both Eddington and Britain's Astronomer Royal, Sir Frank Dyson, the cash-depleted UK government amazingly agreed to send one expedition to Brazil and another to Principe, off the west coast of Africa, to observe a total eclipse on May 29, 1919.

That September, Einstein received a telegram informing him that every prediction he'd calculated using his theories proved accurate, and by October, he was a luminary among his peers in Europe. Einstein thought that would be the extent of his celebrity.

Not for long. On November 6, Dyson read the expeditions' results to a joint session of the Royal Society and the Royal Astronomical Society, after which Royal Society president, J. J. Thomson—the guy who discovered the electron—called Einstein's work "one of the most momentous, if not the most momentous, pronouncements of human thought." The following morning, the *Times of London* shouted "REVOLUTION IN SCIENCE" from its headline, and below it, "New Theory of the Universe. Newtonian Ideas Overthrown."

Nearly a decade and a half after his *annus mirabilis*, or "year of miracles," Albert Einstein's ideas began to enter the mainstream, making him the least likely of international superstars. His proposal that space and time are interwoven into one continuum called "space-time" ignited new conversations within and even outside the scientific community, and the world wanted to know more. Could an event taking place for one observer really happen at another time for someone else? It seemed to millions around the world that a light switch had been flipped, illuminating the foundations of our very existence, causing us to question that which we'd taken for granted since crawling out of the primordial soup.

And so the sight of the mailman in this first year of fame was met with dread. "I have been so swamped with questions, invitations, challenges," Einstein wrote in a letter to a friend, "that I dream that I am burning in Hell and that the postman is the Devil eternally roaring at me, throwing new bundles of letters at my head because I have not yet answered the old ones." He couldn't possibly answer all of them, nor could he comprehend what intrigued scientists and laypeople alike. "I never understood why the theory of relativity with its concepts and problems so far removed from practical life should for so long have met with a lively, or indeed passionate, resonance among broad circles of the public," he wrote decades later. "What could have produced this great and persistent psychological effect? I never yet heard a truly convincing answer to this question."

Einstein once mused, "The only reason for time is so that everything doesn't happen at once," and while he was the first to break time down into a fabric that binds physics and philosophy, evidence and experience, he wasn't the first to attempt to deconstruct it. Of David Hume's *A Treatise of Human Nature*, released in 1738, he wrote, "It is very well possible that without these philosophical studies I would not have arrived at the solution." Of course, the ponderance of time had been a pursuit of philosophers, poets, and the spiritual for millennia before these physicists. Proceeding chronologically, the Tao Te Ching claimed, "There is a time to live and a time to die but never to reject the moment" a few hundred years before Buddha told us, "The trouble is, you think you have time." The Hindu Bhagavad Gita observed, "I am time, the destroyer of all; I have come to consume the world," and the Christian Bible asked, "What is your life? For you are a mist that appears for a little time and then vanishes." The Jewish Talmud asserted, "The best preacher is the heart; the best teacher is time; the best book is the world; the best friend is God," and the Koran told readers, "Allah vowed by ʿA r—which is time—because of its wonders, for within it good and bad matters occur, health and illness, richness and poverty, and because its value and preciousness cannot be measured against anything else." Next, the Japanese Shinto put it sharply, "Time flies like an arrow." Even the wise sage Dr. Seuss posed the question that's plagued the ages: "How did it get so late so soon?"

TIME: THE ULTIMATE LUXURY

I wish Albert were alive to see what we have at our fingertips, where it actually does feel like everything is happening at once. For the generations who grew up charting technological advancements in decades, the modern hyperloop of integrated technologies, scientists, engineers, money, everyware computing, open-source code, cheap hardware, and an impatient audience have amounted to a purring flywheel that's turning faster by the hour. Through the years, I've told my teams that the ultimate luxury is time because you don't know when yours, or the customer's, is up.

I wrote earlier that money is the most popular currency, information the most powerful, and loyalty the amplifier. Time is unique in that it's the only finite currency. It is, as the Koran stated, precious. Jeff Bezos knows this implicitly, and I firmly believe that his worship at the altar of the time currency is one more main key to Amazon's success. For decades, he invested every dollar he could back into the business to reduce time-to-goal for customer and company alike. Free two-day Prime shipping and two-hour Prime Now delivery? Done. Kiva robots in the fulfillment centers moving merchandise to the humans instead of the other way around? Check. Miles of conveyor belts laden with lasers in those centers automatically sorting thousands of parcels an hour? Bingo. Amazon Go stores without a checkout line and automatic payment upon departure? Yep. Kindle e-readers downloading a 500-page title in eight seconds? You betcha. Alexa devices that do your bidding without having to find a machine and type a query? Done and done.

Bezos is known to be a stickler for time—primarily that of the customer. As I mentioned before, your company can't be fast on the outside if it isn't fast on the inside. It was rumored when I was at Amazon that the engineers working on the first Amazon Echo device had gotten its processing and information-retrieval time down to 25 milliseconds as launch day loomed. Impressive right? Unacceptable, at least to this CEO. We heard he set a goal of 12 milliseconds and wouldn't budge. Somehow in the end, they found a way. If you have access to an Alexa device and a Siri-enabled device, ask them both the same question and stopwatch the difference. I've recorded on average the Alexa task is completed at least twice as fast. Every millisecond counts at Amazon, and their smart speaker market share proves it out.

To compound the point, in *The Everything Store: Jeff Bezos and the Age of Amazon*, Brad Stone recounts an executive meeting with VP of Customer Service, Bill Price, in attendance. It was during the fourth quarter, which Amazonians call "peak," and Bezos was curious about call center hold times. These daily Q4 meetings are nicknamed "war rooms," and everyone in corporate worldwide—including we in Advertising—holds them. Everything is evaluated in these gatherings, and you had better come with data to support anything you want to prove, disprove, defend, or change. According to Stone's account, Mr. Price did not have his data. When Bezos asked what hold times were running at this, the most critical time of year, Price responded that they were less than one minute. "Really? Let's see," replied Bezos. Some of the participants told the author that the next four and a half minutes were "interminable." As jolly holiday music emanated from the speakerphone, Bezos all but turned red with fury. When a service rep finally answered, he blurted, "I'm just calling to check," and hung up. While I can only imagine what ensued with Price and the whole room afterward, I don't have to guess that Bezos considers the customer's time priceless.

In orders of magnitude, time is the most valuable currency. The best brands know this and nimbly navigate challenges internally to instantly gratify externally. Yes, customers today are less patient than ever, but if you think that's going to change, you're sadly mistaken. It's only going to intensify as everyone, every machine, hell, every *surface* with a sensor embedded in it is crunching data faster today in response to a command than it did yesterday. For brands, just as in the wild, the slow are the first to die.

After all, the last time I checked, the human mortality rate is hanging right around 100 percent, so job number one for companies is to make much of time on behalf of their customers.

CHAPTER 14

———

Time and the Customer

"Brevity, the lifeblood of levity."

—UNCLE MILT

Not sure about you, but no one's ever greeted me with "Happy Deathday!" and thrown a party in my honor. We celebrate the day of our birth annually, but there's one box on the calendar that marks exact years until we slip the surly bonds of earth to touch the face of God. This mystery day lives way down in the cockles of our minds, manifesting itself first in impatience, then real anger in long checkout lines, and finally road rage or worse. It claws at us, mocks us with its temporal secret, drives us to do things we typically wouldn't. As we move through adult life, we know the day draws closer and are forced to reluctantly shake hands with it every time we lose a loved one. We are walking, ticking time limits.

In every interaction with your brand, your customers are

already paying you with their money, information, and loyalty. But their time too? Now you're getting expensive. Online and off, they're performing tasks in pursuit of their happiness—sometimes your brand is invited to take part—but since time is the only finite currency, they can't earn time like they can the other currencies. They can only reduce what they spend and are innately drawn like moths to a flame to anything which lowers that cost, precisely because they don't know how much they have left. It is the essence of what Shakespeare described in *Hamlet*'s "To be, or not to be" soliloquy as to "shuffle off this mortal coil."

Remember, Einstein taught us that time was relative to the observer. The activities that take our time, it stands to reason, hold the power to elongate or shrink the appearance of how much we're spending. Three hours watching your favorite football team are surely not the same 180 minutes to someone serving life in prison. The clock says it is, but the mind doesn't. Time does fly when you're having fun, and it crawls when you're in a boardroom with Bezos next to a speakerphone on hold. That's precisely why great advertising resonates, and the bad is reviled or just outright ignored. We are forced to pay for linear TV content with our time by consuming ads, but that's changing. As of 2017, we willingly exchanged 14:37 of advertisements for every 45:23 of entertainment, down 14 percent from 2016. As we've predicted for years, OTT boxes and DVRs have begun to take their toll on traditional advertising.

What are people doing instead with that time? Why going online of course, where the perception of time changes. Witness the rise of the six-second ad, now the accepted standard of social media. In the pixel-rich world of only everything in an instant, digital expands time. By how much? Judging by the advertisement length of six seconds online versus 30 seconds on TV, it appears to be a factor of five. That's because if I'm in a social environment like Instagram, ads are far more intrusive than on television, where I ignore them while looking at my phone or getting something to eat. In aggregate, if you believe Microsoft's *Attention Spans Research Report* from 2015, the time we're able to focus on a task has dropped from 12 seconds to eight, which is lower than that of a goldfish's nine seconds.

Even though I do firmly believe our expectations for what we should receive per time spent have risen, I have to call Brussels Sprouts on the Microsoft report, which cited the numbers from another source named Statistic Brain, whom the BBC attempted to contact for verification but were unsuccessful. The goldfish bit makes for great headlines, but without hard evidence, I can't subscribe to it. What I can share with you is that all the major social platforms recommend in their best practices to brands and agencies that the main message should be communicated within an ad's first two seconds. That tells me all I need to know. Unlike TV, ads online are rarely full-screen, which means the customer need merely divert her gaze elsewhere on the page or just keep scrolling.

That's why it's a major challenge to earn even a 0.5 percent click-through rate on these things. There's just too much competition for her already-miniscule digital attention.

Where advertising and relevant audience targeting are seen as a bit more of an equitable exchange for the customer's time is Amazon. According to a Comscore study from March 2018, Americans spent 22.6 billion minutes on the site in December 2017, 36% more than the combined total of 16.6 billion spent on the next nine-largest e-commerce destinations. There, as I described earlier, customers are served ads designed to help them make better decisions according to their purchase and browsing history. The more time a visitor spends in the Amazon universe, the smarter the system gets for what they'll see next time.

TIME IN THE TECHONOMY

What Bezos knew way back at the beginning is that the first service to save a customer time and money using information would drive loyalty. Think of the time saved when comparison shopping online versus off. The consumer's innate desire to get the most out of her limited minutes has led directly to the power reduction of brands—not competition from Amazon, as many industry experts claim.

Consider websites that not only load slowly but are not responsive and are poorly designed. The importance of humanistic design cannot be overstated. Great user experience (UX) designers with real empathy for the customer are worth their weight in palladium, and a site is only as good as the usefulness of information the customer receives per unit of time, which is why personalization makes a real difference. Not only is a digital environment that recognizes you and your history more effective, it saves you considerable amounts of time by predicting your next move. Even if it guesses correctly only once out of five interactions, that's still time saved. With machine learning, the chances of accurately forecasting a customer's next click or tap increases with every visit. Furthermore, empathically designed sites that offer a consistent on- or offline product really earn time back for the customer to invest elsewhere. For instance, I know J.Crew clothing fits me perfectly, so I don't even need to gather the sensory information of trying on their merchandise in-store. I'm on and off their site in under a minute, and they will have my business forever because of it. A well-designed, consistent product and experience effectively become the "elite member" counters at the car rental office or TSA PreCheck at the airport.

What artificial intelligence is about to do for customer service will be nothing short of staggering for saving customers time. We already have chat bots and some voice-enabled services, but they're not comprehensive or quick enough to fully replace humans just yet. Until then, we're stuck listening to Muzak as the recorded voice tells us every 15 seconds how important our call is to them and that the next available representative *yada yada*. Guess how long average Americans spend on hold during their lifetimes. According to mobile advertising analytics firm Marchex, it's a whopping 43 days. It won't be long, however, until we have no-hold, on-demand call center skills on our voice-enabled speakers which are guaranteed to be the telegraph to that industry's Pony Express. Spoken queries will search cloud-based indices and correctly respond in milliseconds, saving the customer time and the brand money, earning it higher loyalty and revenue through the power of instant information. At last, will we say goodbye forever to whole afternoons wasted at the DMV? Man I hope so.

Just look at Rocket Mortgage from Detroit-based Quicken Loans for a marketplace-busting example. Leveraging automation and real design thinking, the home mortgage application has transformed from stacks of forms laboriously filled out in triplicate and faxed to a human at a bank into a simple question-and-answer process that yields an approval in ten minutes on your smartphone. Innovation like Rocket Mortgage has propelled the lender past dinosaur banks like Wells Fargo and Bank of America into the number one spot, accounting for 6 percent of mortgages in the US. In the fourth quarter of 2017 alone, Quicken issued $25 billion worth of them. Saving the customer time is the key to what company founder Dan Gilbert told *TechCrunch* will do to the mortgage space what the iPhone did to the handset industry.

SPEED SELLS

Customer time saved is one of Amazon's silver bullets. Beyond the two-day Prime and two-hour Prime Now delivery services, Amazon sees selection as the ultimate time-saver too. When a customer can find everything in one place, the time needed to self-fulfill her needs is greatly minimized.

"I very frequently get the question: 'What's going to change in the next 10 years?'" Bezos was once quoted. "I almost never get the question: 'What's not going to change in the next 10 years?' And I submit to you that that second question is actually the more important of the two—because you can build a business strategy around the things that are stable in time...In our retail business, we know that customers want low prices, and I know that's going to be true 10 years from now. They want fast delivery; they want vast selection...It's impossible to imagine a future 10 years from now where a customer comes up and says, 'Jeff I love Amazon; I just wish the prices were a little higher,' or 'I love Amazon; I just wish you'd deliver a little more slowly.' Impossible."

I can't count how many times I've heard people say they shop Amazon not for the low prices but the delivery speed. Saving your customer time is the ultimate sign of respect, which expedites your journey to loyalty and ultimately joyalty. Startups looking for quick wins in their early years should take heed and prioritize saving their customers' time as the primary objective. It was precisely the fuel Amazon used to move from book- to everything-retail, and how a 33-year-old mortgage company left a 166-year old bank in the dust. As Ben Franklin wrote in 1789, "In this world nothing can be said to be certain, except death and taxes." We're all going to find ourselves on a worm's menu someday. Treating the customer's time as consciously as your own is the fastest route to brand glory.

CHAPTER 15

Time and the Brand

"If you're early, you're either genius or lucky, both virtuous traits. The late are forgotten."

—UNCLE MILT

We know customers spend a lot of time on hold. Do brand owners have an equivalent? According to a 2014 study performed by Bain & Company, senior executives spend, on average, two of every five business days stuck in meetings. In 2017, *Harvard Business Review* cited research from *MIT Sloan Management Review* a decade earlier that meetings have grown in both duration and frequency over the previous half-century, from less than 10 hours in the 1960s to an average of nearly 23 hours a week, a 130 percent increase. Worse, those stats don't even take into account the time needed to prepare for meetings or debrief afterward.

There are a number of differing views on just how many

meetings corporate Americans attend every day and how much they cost. The US Bureau of Labor Statistics doesn't have anything recent enough to be relevant to today's climate, but according to *Inc.* in 2017, "There are between 36 and 56 million meetings in the United States every day, and the lost productivity that comes from ineffective meetings costs businesses anywhere from $70–$283 billion each year." An earlier *Inc.* article claims that of the 1,400 professionals who responded to a survey by online collaboration and project management company Wrike, "When asked if they leave company meetings knowing what the next action item is, only 54 percent said 'yes.' The rest answered, 'some of the time,' 'rarely,' or 'never.'"

Who pays for all that? The customer, of course. If yours is a cover-your-ass culture where everyone on earth is invited to the call so as to insulate the meeting-holder from any responsibility should things go awry down the road, your operational expenditure is a balloon filled with hot air and little to show for it. That dynamic breaks the rules of the money currency. When people aren't frugal with others' time, the brand begins to tell a sluggish story of bloat and expense. It seeps through the conference room walls to the outside world in the form of higher prices, longer reaction times, and fewer innovations—certain to displease the customer (not to mention the beloved shareholder).

I mentioned in chapter 6 that "we run lean" is a commonly

heard phrase at Amazon when discussing the approach to staffing. When there aren't layers upon layers of staff to throw at a problem, meetings have to be time-frugal because there simply aren't that many people available, and those who can join are already pretty busy. Just imagine what you could do with your piece of that $70–283 billion wasted in meetings each year. Don't get me wrong—there are lean companies, and then there are bare-bones. I'm not espousing threadbare staffing either, where everyone burns out and quits, at which point millions of dollars' worth of institutional knowledge and investment walk out one day and never come back. I *am* saying, though, that with too many people, critical actions like approvals and product delivery simply take a lot longer.

To solve for this, Bezos is known for his "two-pizza team" rule, which stipulates that any group of employees assigned to collaborate on a solution should never be so large that two pizzas couldn't feed them. Communication improves and speed increases when you have no more than, say, six people tasked with an assignment. To demonstrate the point, take a two-pizza team of five people and count the maximum possible one-on-one connections between the individual participants. Four for each member means there are a maximum of 20 two-person communications channels. Now double the size of that group to 10, and the number of one-to-one connections more than quadruples to 90. Just as in machinery, the more moving parts a system has, the higher the probability it will break. Think about it: do you have more meaningful conversations when you host a small dinner party or when you're the bride at a massive wedding reception? Running lean is less expensive and more nimble, and it also prevents the overconfidence borne from "safety in numbers" as well as loss of participation, after more and more voices enter the room and crowd out the lower-ranking and introverted members.

Listening to each other as much as American employees do devours time to spend on the customer and, ya know, doing actual work. The "always-on innovation cycle" I mentioned earlier depends on these small teams remaining free of handcuffs to hit aggressive deadlines. Because everyone has goals and programs, pretty much anyone you meet at the company will excuse you for the inability to attend a noncritical conference call. The one important meeting that my and no doubt hundreds of teams attended every morning were called "scrums." If you're unfamiliar with the Agile method so popular in software development, this is when a project manager and all team members gather (usually standing at a whiteboard so it proceeds efficiently and ends quickly) to discuss the status of where they are in their "sprint," or incremental, iterative work sequence. That short stand-up—typically no longer than 15 minutes—was more productive than most of the others I'd have all day.

THE TEAM AND TIME

Another area where I think most brand owners could stand to reassess how they spend their time is hiring. In chapter 2, I detailed bar-raising and how the practice of ensuring every new hire is better than half the existing organization continually elevates the performance of the team and, by extension, the entire company. It takes a lot of time to do it properly, but it's obviously for the right reason. Think about the interview process where you work. Are there values or principals that inform your questions and are used in evaluating the candidate's fit, or is it a popularity contest? Are there debriefs? Are the conversations captured in any way? Are you spending enough time on the faces of your company's and brand's future? If you're not sure, the answer's no. That doesn't mean you can't get on it ASAP. No core leadership principals? Start a program tomorrow to create them first at the company level and then departmentally. No interview question library? Program that too. Naturally, HR might push back, so offer to take the lead and work alongside them to get it done. Those artifacts will help streamline and save time on what is one of the most important aspects of any business.

Relatedly, how much time does your organization spend examining your customer experience and being honest about its shortcomings? Weekly, we held "Walk the Store" sessions, before which we would browse the Amazon universe, take in the branded experiences our teams built as they appeared in live environments, just as a customer would. This is not

unlike Bezos's real-time check of the call center's hold duration. We'd all arrive with screenshots of what we found, and
the group would discuss what we could do better. This wasn't
a blame-and-shame session; rather, we would discover hic-
cups that we couldn't have known until we saw them live, like
the juxtaposition of two unrelated ad units that, in situation,
looked like a futuristic gun on a video game package aimed
at a baby's head in a diaper ad. An organization of humble,
customer-centric people take this seriously, and it was a productive, customer-first expenditure of 60 minutes.

BEAT THE HEAT

It's far better that you do it yourselves before your customers
do so for you. In chapter 8, I discussed the Net Promoter
Score (NPS), the industry-standard evaluation of customer
satisfaction. In its Net Promoter Score Benchmark Study 2018,
customer experience research firm Temkin Group analyzed
the NPS of more than 340 companies from 20 industries
based on a survey of 10,000 American consumers. Scores
range 100 points, from –20 to 80, and for the second year
in a row, USAA set the pace for the whole study with a 65
(its maritime competitor, Navy Federal Credit Union, was a
close second in the Insurance Carriers category). USAA, a
company of military members for military personnel and their
families is the model of customer loyalty. At the opposite end
of the spectrum sat the TV/Internet Service vertical, scores
for which spanned from a high of 19 to a low of –16 for an

industry average of 0 points. The −16 belonged to the one and only Comcast, which made the news in 2015 for, among other things, sending bills addressed to two angry customers who'd spent time on the phone with customer service as "Super Bitch Bauer" and "Asshole Brown."

Comcast's reputation as one of the most hated companies in America is not likely to change hands for some time. Refusing to cancel dissatisfied customers' accounts and, you guessed it, underfunded call centers known for eternal hold times will do well to exterminate a brand in time. Another repeat bottom-dweller, Time Warner Cable, was forced to spend a year and sizable sums to rebrand itself to Spectrum in the hopes of recovering from a generation of terrible brand equity. Indeed, the hours of making hard evaluations of your product and customer experience are time well spent.

THE KNOWLEDGE OF LONDON

Brands that spend time in the right ways create strong bonds with customers. Loyalty is, after all, merely a measure of devotion over time. To demonstrate, I'll now turn to an analogy that'll seem strange at first, but stick with me. When I lived in London, I learned about the legend of "The Knowledge." The Knowledge of London is the name Transport for London (TfL) bestowed upon the transportation world's deepest-dive training program back in 1865, long before the oddly beautiful black cabs and double-decker buses came to define the capital's streets.

Because London's thoroughfares have changed minimally since then, the Knowledge hasn't been updated much either. Candidates, known as "Knowledge Boys" (and the occasional "Girl"), spend upwards of four years studying every inch of pavement and cobblestone within a six-mile radius of Charing Cross in Central London. During their years of Knowledge acquisition, the Boys and Girls cover upwards of 20,000 miles on mopeds in every type of weather and traffic imaginable. They're easy to recognize for the standing clipboard affixed to their handlebars. (I loved walking up to them and rooting them on with a "You can do it, mate!" to which they would exhale dramatically and shake their heads with eyes wide open as if to say, "Dunno, mate.")

Indoors, they spend untold hours drawing lines on massive laminated wall maps to work out the fastest route between thousands of "points of interest" on Central London's 25,000 tangled streets—hotels, train stations, hospitals, houses of worship, top restaurants, concert halls, movie theaters, you name it. During these years they're summoned to tests called "appearances," of which there are around 15 according to the conversations I had with these men and women. At an appearance, candidates are asked to meticulously detail the most efficient route between any two points. One instructor was known to throw two darts at a map for total randomness.

These appearances were by all accounts terrifying, and the object of their universal dread until their examiners ascertained they were knowledgeable enough and called them up to the big leagues.

I bring up these proud folks here in the "Time" section for good reason: whenever I asked them how they liked driving cabs in one of the world's great cities, they would gush for the entire ride about how much they love it. I mean they really, *really* love it. "After all that time it took to learn the Knowledge, I wouldn't do anything else," one told me. "If I won the lottery, I'd still do it, just not the late shift." Note he said, "After all that time it took." Time and a lot of elbow grease combined for pride in and *true love* of something, in this case, a profession. The experience alters them professionally, sure, but also, it seemed, spiritually. And just think, all of this in an era of GPS and sat-navs. (Warning: do not bring up Uber with these Londoners lest you receive a stream of vitriol for their less-dedicated cousins.)

The moral of the Knowledge is that ordinary people can learn to fall in love with anything when they put in the time. It's why we wistfully look back to our high school, university, or military days—formative, typically four-year periods in our lives spent working to achieve a certification of some kind. When we earn it, we are forever transformed, and usually wouldn't change the years working toward it for anything. Certainly, the Knowledge is an extreme example of time dedicated to complex subject matter, and multiple studies show that the London cab driver's hippocampus, the brain region dedicated to things like spatial memory and navigation, is larger than the general public's.

Ask yourself, when it comes to your customer, how big is your brand's hippocampus? How much time do you spend learning every single detail you can about the customer as the Knowledge Boys and Girls did with those enormous, twisted London maps?

MI TIEMPO, SU TIEMPO

Let me finish with a note that brands can "receive" time, too, in the form of hours they don't need to spend to achieve a result. Earned media is a prime example. When a brand's evangelists and the press share their message for it, that amplifies the money and time it has already spent on earning new customers and advancing the stories in existing customers' heads. Workflow efficiencies count as well. At Amazon, this takes shape in the "Innovate, Iterate, Automate" motto I presented to my teams. Collaboration tools were of high importance during my time there and the object of countless programs, making it easier and faster for more and more brains to attack a problem. Another good way brands can get time back is by exchanging the money currency for intellectual property acquisition. If you have the means and it makes sense by the customer, why spend scores of man-years developing your own fulfillment robots when you can buy Kiva and be done with it?

No matter your area of business, when you save yourself time, you save the customer's time. She will naturally gravitate toward your offering without processing the decision because the human mind is hardwired to placate its innate countdown clock. Albert Einstein, whose breaths ran out on April 18, 1955 from an abdominal aortic aneurysm, showed us that time is relative to the observer. Ask a teenage boy and a woman in hospice what today means to them and you'll know. Sounds grim for a business book, but all of us have a deathday looming. We know this, yet live every day doing our futile best to outrun it. Treat your business as a time machine for your customer, and your brand will outlive us all.

In Closing

"Desire and lack are human constants. Great brands artfully remind us of both."

—UNCLE MILT

So there you have it. Money, information, loyalty, and time represent the four primal ingredients the wisest implicitly grasp and leverage to survive and ultimately thrive. They are co-responsible for empires, nations, families, companies, and, yes, brands rising and falling. They start wars and sue for peace. They make for pleasure, despair, wholeness, and deficiency. They are the final inward and outward signals of this mortal coil. And they've made it clear they're not going anywhere—not in your lifetime anyway.

The four currencies are also why Amazon has dumbfounded the business world in less than a quarter-century. I hope my insights into how the company abides by and integrates them into its everyday fabric help you not only see the company in a new way but as a model you can adapt to your business to drive brand discipline and, later, excellence. Apply the ideologies of leadership principles, goals, programs, long-term over short-term, fail fast, Day 1, the empty chair, raising the bar, the Andon cord, and customer-first humility to your daily work. It won't happen overnight, but you will see transformative results. Challenge yourself and those around you. Become an Amazon of One and others will follow. They'll be inclined to. It's in their DNA.

When I sat down to write *Brand Currency*, I didn't know where to start. That was familiar because it's exactly how I felt at the start of every program I led at Amazon. Over time, I learned that's just the way thinking big is supposed to feel, and it always works out in the end if I just keep the customer top of mind. I was a proverbial robotic vacuum cleaner, bumping into walls and table legs until I broke free into open space, collecting the dust of data and new ideas. Face it: you're going to fail. The bigger the idea, the more botches await. Thomas Edison generated more than 10,000 prototypes before arriving at a commercially viable light bulb, about which he proudly claimed, "I have not failed 10,000 times. I have not failed once. I have succeeded in proving that those 10,000 ways will not work. When I have eliminated the ways that will not work, I will find the way that will work." Are you as intelligent and patient as the most prolific inventor in American history? Maybe you are, maybe you aren't. Either way, just get started. In the proper context, the business of failing is a total blast. Embrace it, laugh at it, and share it. Just don't repeat the same fail twice. Then you're simply wasting time, the most valuable currency of all.

On the subject of Amazon, let's not sugarcoat this book. That company is hardly perfect. It's merely a collective of hundreds of thousands of human beings as flawed as the rest of us. However, when that box containing ice skates for your niece lands on your doorstep faster than if you made time for a shopping trip—and at a lower cost—it can sometimes feel perfect. No organization anywhere is faultless, but that doesn't mean you can't try to stumble upon excellence along the way.

Amazon's success is not by chance. It was all but assured by design in 1994. Bezos learned from his D. E. Shaw days that grand ambition needs a structure or it's destined for the realm of irrational exuberance, of which people quickly grow weary and then quit. Data, just another word for "customer," provides that framework. Gather as much as you can and let it help you make better decisions. As a professional creative for two and a half decades now, I started my career looking down my nose at data. "That's for the nerds," I thought. "Analysts and product developers need the numbers. Real creatives go on instinct and experience." Bull pucky. Instinct is shaped by experience, and the numbers can provide invaluable parameters by showing where the crap is located so you don't step in it. Information, the most powerful currency, wins every argument, breaks every tie, drives loyalty, saves us all money and time.

When I left the traditional ad agency space in 1996 to concentrate on digital, I didn't know then that I was drawn innately to those numbers. People said I was crazy to leave the cushy world of TV spots and magazine ads, and I told them all they were the crazy ones. "Like it or not, this is where the world is going. How do you know if your work is actually effective?" They couldn't answer then and still can't now. Offline attribution models are built on lofty assumptions, and until we all have chips in our brains, they'll almost certainly remain that way. (The rise of digital television is helping close the gap, but we have a long way to go for media like out-of-home and print.) Years later, when I left the digital agency space for Amazon in 2012, they openly questioned my sanity again. By then, I was sufficiently self-aware to understand that the data were exactly what I was after. Who could have more than Amazon? With it, you find out just how good you really are in short order. At a company serving millions of pageviews a minute, one discovers exactly how that headline or promise resonates (or not) with the customer at scale.

Working in an environment rife with data grounds you on a moment-to-moment basis. Sometimes it can be dispiriting. Excitedly watching a team spend a few months building a branded experience that elicits a ho-hum response from the customer is never a good feeling. No one likes rejection, particularly when a major advertiser is paying for it, but at least we were equipped with the coordinates for where to attack and fix the problem. We would rinse and repeat until we got it right. In my early days there, it felt like "That didn't work last time" was my personal tagline, but because it came from a good place, there was no shame. It's always Day 1. And hey, on the bright side, after enough missteps, the quality of your work inherently begins to increase as your muscle memory and creative reflexes sharpen.

Of course, all of the above can amount to wishful thinking without goals and programs supported by data-capture and analysis. The evidence of one's effort, reviewed by leadership every week, prevents him or her from lapsing into unhealthy habits, or worse, laziness. If you don't have any goals—professional or otherwise—start by writing one down right now. It's easy and free of charge. Already have goals? Commit them to a program and tie it to the four currencies. Combine them into multicurrency events to boost the program's impact. Implement and outwardly communicate your program to colleagues and even family so you'll hold yourself to it. Feel free to fail fast on behalf of the customer without penalty, capture the reasons why, and spread the news so your partners don't repeat it. Collect data to prove that your actions and their results are tangible. Evaluate on these data and actively offer them to your superiors and coworkers. Surround yourself with people who are better than half of all others on your team and social circle to continue to raise the bar of your workplace and life. Keep going until you get your light bulb. Only 9,999 to go.

As more and more companies learn (some the hard way) how to maximize the four currencies for their customer and, by extension, themselves, I believe we will see an unprecedented shift toward corporate responsibility and transparency, and away from malfeasance. There will always be bad apples, but with the consumer's sizable and growing power over brands, the days are numbered for those organizations not firmly in her corner, listening keenly. Blockchain will permanently and publicly preserve every corporate move and, assuming the tech has been built with the best, bias-free intentions, there will be nowhere for the ne'er-do-wells to hide. Plus, we all know the traditional model is dead as a doornail. The consumer doesn't live in a purchase funnel anymore, moving from awareness to consideration on down to conversion, repurchase, and loyalty. Rather, she's in a loop, where endless selection, price wars, last-mile logistics, and technologies like augmented reality, voice-activated shopping, and personalization enable her to imagine exactly what she wants, find it in minutes, and have it in hours—not just blindly accept what's on offer. Her world is not supply- but demand-driven, and she wields a gavel in the shape of a smartphone. We have no choice but to do her bidding.

You can resist or dive in. If you elect to ignore the neon writing on the wall, commence rearranging deck chairs on the Titanic at once. Those who choose the latter will flip their marketing budgets from heavy-up advertising (talking) to mostly community-building (listening). The smartest companies will establish social mission control centers dedicated solely to tracking customer sentiment and the language customers use to describe their products and services. That language will proactively inform their brand's verbal identity and be deployed when engaging with the audience. They will hand over the keys of their brand to enthusiasts and empower them to influence friends on their behalf, however they want to do it. They will overinvest in customer service. They will invite the customer to innovate products and services alongside their developers for a new level of co-ownership and transparency. They will break down the internal silos that separate the owners of their customer touchpoints. They will be committed to vigorously seeking problem areas instead of burying their heads in the sand. They will encourage open dialogue that turns bad customer experiences into great ones in real time. They will see everyone around them as a customer and empower each employee to offer assistance without taking the time to ask permission. They will focus on helping customers make the best decisions possible, not selling. They will hire and promote humble people who accept that it's not about them. They will let go of the egotistical and the know-it-alls. They will convince their shareholders to be patient. And they will enjoy four currency balance sheets that are firmly in the black.

Whether you're a startup or a leviathan that's been around for 150 years doesn't matter. The universe is indifferent. Implement this approach immediately and start earning and exchanging money, information, loyalty, and time instead of wasting them.

Now that this book is out, you'd better get moving.

Acknowledgments

Limitless appreciation goes to:

James Timberlake, Karla Bynum, Jessica Burdg, Emily Gindlesparger, Erin Tyler, Meghan McCracken, and Zach Obront at Scribe Media.

Scott Hines, Bobby Figueroa, Michael Dwan, and Paul Kotas for the opportunity to join Amazon and build cool stuff for its customers.

My Amazon teammates in New York, London, Munich, Paris, Milan, Tokyo, Toronto, Los Angeles, Bangalore, Palo Alto, and Seattle, from whom I absorbed everything you just read: Cecilia Ambros, Daniel Apt, Aanchal Bharti, Tony Biaggne, Daisy Binks, Gerald Blee, Kelly Bork, Gary Brosnan, Baron Brown, David Buckley, Thomas Caliman, Alessandro Camedda, Jude Carter-Edwards, Sébastien Casaert, John Cathey-Roberts, Mark Centoducati, Alex Chamas, Jordan Chamberlain,

Madeline Chan, Maud Charon, Michael Chase, Regan Coleman, Guthrie Collin, Bob Coon, Neil Coxhill, Munish Dabas, Seth Dallaire, Nancy DeRobles, Edouard Dinichert, Dom Dressler, Josh Eisenman, Leanne Farnham, Kate Fetty, Tom Fochetta, Adam Fournier, Cameron Frantz, Chris Fuller, Jason Galep, Britt Gannon, Katharina Ganzer, Silvia Gehrer, Heike Geier, Lauren Giaccobo, John Gill, Camilla Giulietti, Richard Glazier, Kyle Golder, Shira Gordon, Jeremi Gorman, Linnae Goswami, Leigh Graham, Johnny Greges, Christoph Groß, Paul Hackwell, Allison Heim, John Herd, Jimmy Hickey, Caleb Hill, Alex Hole, Stefan Höss, Josh Hudson, Xerxes Irani, Casey Jamison, Garrett Jamison, Yogesh Juneja, Michael Kazantzis, Keenan Kelly, Thomas Knight, Richard Kirk, Takuji Koide, Anna Kravcova, Felix Kühner, Greg Kujda, Kenny Kushner, Steve Landau, Mickael Larcheveque, Daniel Lindo, Frazer Locke, Michael Lowenstern, Annie Loye, Duncan Mackie, Scott Maize, Janna Mamar, Mark Mannino, Hiroko Matsui, Jon Mawer, Sally Medina, Pradeep Menon, Philip Missler, Yuri Miura, Daniel Modell, Matt Morton, Prashant Mudhalkar, Ben Myhre, Tzur Nehushtan, Indro Neri, Wade Neumeister, Keelin O'Brien, Elton Ollerhead, Marcus Pape, Sunita Patradoon Ho, John Percival, Lauren Pergola, Tina Perry, Roberta Piancazzo, Bill Pearce, Stephanie Porter, Jonathan Post, Shaun Post, Damiano Povoleri, Charles-Henri Putz, Vijay Raju, Harry Reffold, Pierre Reme, Melissa Riccardi, James Robinson, Brian Rogers, Julian Rost, Samson Samuel, Michaela Scholz, Martin Schrittenloher, Tara Scott, Jamie Scythes, Sunao Shirase, Amanda Singleton, Sonny Sisto, LaShaun Skillings,

Alexandra Smith, Kevin Snell, Felicia Soto, Kenji Sugino, Young Sun, Chiori Suzuki, Matt Swan, Robin Sweers, Michele Tagliavini, Phil Taylor, Justin Thomas, Lubo Todorov, Cassy Toomey, Mari Tsukamoto, Chadia Toumani, Julien Tourneux, Joey Tuminello, David Ulloa, Salmeh Vakilian, Ru Vallury, Aaron Vradenburgh, Louise Wainwright, Cindy Walker, Marc Wallowy, Anselm Weier, Desiree West, Mark Williamson, Corby Winer, Jonathan Wood, Tae Yamashita, Hidetomo Yokosuka, Marianna You, Miry Yun, and Zibin Yuan.

Artie Isaac, Laura Sommers, and Michael Regan for giving me my first agency job at Young Isaac in Columbus, Ohio.

Sue Karlin and her agency SUKA Creative for everything they've done for me over the years.

Dianne Wilkins, Chris Gokiert, and Conor Brady for the opportunity to join Critical Mass before my days at Amazon and rejoin afterward, for your support of my writing this book, and for creating a culture of customer obsession, humility, creativity, and intelligence unmatched in the agency world.

And Brett Spearing, Hunter Harrison, and Kathryn Reffold, whom the world lost far too soon.

In loving memory of my grandparents.

Thank you.

About the Author

After 16 years with New York's digital ad agencies, **STEVE SUSI** joined Amazon Advertising as its first creative director in the New York City office in 2012, where his teams would deliver original brand experiences on behalf of hundreds of brands and millions of customers worldwide. In 2014, he became its first group creative director globally and, two years later, first executive creative director, moving to London to lead creative operations across Europe, Asia, and Canada. In 2016, he was recognized for his contribution to the company's technology by receiving the first Amazon Inventor Award granted to Advertising outside the US for patent-pending innovation.

A proud graduate of Subiaco Academy and Miami University, Steve lives on Manhattan's Upper West Side.

Made in the USA
Columbia, SC
26 May 2021

38547948R00157